DO YOU FEEL LIKE WRITING?

A Creative Guide to Artistic Confidence

DO YOU FEEL LIKE WRITING?

A Creative Guide to Artistic Confidence

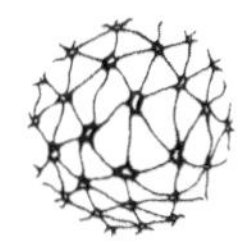

Frankie Rollins

Published by Fifth Brain Collective
ISBN: 979-8-9881937-0-8, paperback
ISBN: 979-8-9881937-1-5, ebook
Printed in the United States of America

Cover design and interior images by Kye Davolt
Design and typesetting by HR Hegnauer
Author photo by Julius Schlosburg

For Eric Aldrich, Sandra Shattuck, and Beth Laking,
the fairy godparents of the fifth brain

Table of Contents

Preface

Many summers ago, I was at a coffee shop writing with my friend, Sandra, a colleague at my teaching job and someone with whom I had just started to have regular writing sessions. I told her a story about how once when I was younger and newly devoted to my writing, I got up for a break. I went to the fridge, and with wonder, found a black ballpoint pen on the shelf next to the milk. I went back to my bedroom, where a makeshift desk was crammed into a corner, and from across the room I could see a block of cheese sitting there, on top of my papers. When I touched the cheese, it was warm. It had been sitting beside me for hours, on top of that door-turned-desk. There were more pens. There was a computer. There were paper drafts of stories and this block of cheese.

I told Sandra that I wished I could know what I was thinking about when I moved from desk to fridge with a pen in my hand. What distracted me when I enacted the exchange, placed the pen on the rungs of the fridge shelf, and lifted the block of cheese? Interrupted by this new vision, I must have floated back to my desk, set down the cheese, picked up a different pen, and written long enough for the cheese to grow warm.

"That goes in the book," Sandra said when I finished telling her this story.

"What book?"

"The book on writing you're going to write someday," she said.

"I'm not writing a book on writing," I said. "What are you talking about?"

For years after I'd gone off on a rant against creative limitations or told a story from my writing life, Sandra would say, "That goes in the book, too."

This is the book that was waiting for me.

After writing through decades of personal upheavals and myriad jobs, and perhaps because of those upheavals and jobs, I've gained many tools to help me write. This book offers these tools, naming and exploring the phenomenon of mixing the conscious and subconscious in generative ways. *Do You Feel Like Writing?* offers metacognitive examinations, insights from other authors, and stories from my experience, as well as inventive writing prompts to help you access your own patterns of imagination and knowledge.

Do You Feel Like Writing? offers ways to sustain a writing life, but it won't be the same way for everyone. This book honors your particular wisdom, your particular instincts. It is creatively, intellectually, emotionally, and socially challenging to make time for writing, but I urge you to do it. I raise some questions for you to answer in this book. Do you believe that you have an imagination particular to you? Do you value your imagination? Do you accept that you have knowledge that only your experiences could create? Do you know what you want from writing? Do you know how to prioritize the time for creativity? Can you give yourself permission to write?

At the end of each chapter, I offer a series of prompts titled "Do You Feel Like Writing?" These are included because I want you to remember that this book is about helping you get your writing done. Approach these exercises with freedom and a sense of play. Squeeze an idea like a grape and find more ideas within. You can always use biographical prompts to explore characters rather than yourself and vice versa. Trust that you have permission. There is no such thing as an imposter writing your sentences. Just you, the writing instrument, and the trustworthy, unconscious part of your imagination that I call the fifth brain.

I am obsessed with making sentences, so this book focuses on prose, which is my main form, but the ideas here are relevant to other types of creativity. You can transform prompts into material for paintings or songs or graffiti or digital art or tattoos or sculpture or ceramics or photography or cartoons or cave paintings. Everyone has a right to create with sentences, poetic lines, paint, clay, pixels, music, and any creative tools as they choose, and everyone has a fifth brain that they can learn to trust.

For more prompts, webinars, and one-on-one coaching,
sign up for the Fifth Brain Collective newsletter at
fifthbraincollective.com.

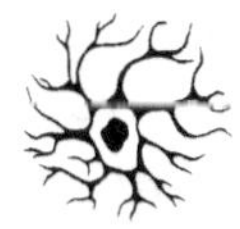

CHAPTER ONE

You Own Your Imagination

Once I was getting ready to move and I found a box full of tiny notebooks from my purses over the years. The notebooks were desiccated from pages torn out, ink-smeared, ratty, and dusty. I almost took the box over to a trash bag without looking inside any of the notebooks. There were handfuls of them with curled edges, a hundred different colors and shapes. They were so light; how could they contain anything meaningful? I opened one and started reading. Sentences snatched from conversations, character sketches, illegible notes scribbled in dark movie theaters. Fervent wishes, lines of poems, epiphanies. Grocery lists. Scraps of real moments translated into fiction. Phone numbers floating without names. What I was going to throw away, this trash, was gathered evidence of my writing mind, my imagination. What I was going to throw away was essentially mine, essentially me.

What evidence will you leave of your imaginative life, of your own particular brain?

One of the reasons we don't inherently know whether to trash or treasure our ideas is because movies and books often portray an artistic person accessing a muse from outside of their body. This implies that the most amazing gifts for a writer come from the outside, rather than the inside. The idea of an outside muse implies that we have no control over our writing, can't access it when we want to, or that we could even lose it. This isn't so. Every writer has a part of their brain working for them during conscious and unconscious hours, gathering, sifting, and sorting. I call this meaning-maker the fifth brain. Your fifth brain belongs to you. It translates the juices of your observations, churns the connections, isolates the truth of what you want to say. It's working inside of you right now. You are the muse you seek.

You may not know, consciously, where to go with an idea, how to write it. But way back there in your fifth brain, there is a little animal part of you formulating the work you need to, want to, must make. In *Becoming a Writer*, Dorothea Brande says writers should "hitch your unconscious mind to your writing arm." Trusting the fifth brain is a way to do that, to trust that what rises in your mind is where you should begin. There's no other factor. You can start there, with your first idea.

The fifth brain is a metaphor for ease of accessing imagination, harnessing material, and trusting in each writer's singularity. The fifth brain works in the unconscious, making connections. When I came up with this metaphor, years ago teaching a creative writing class, I mentioned that a student might trust her fifth brain and was met with half a class of blank stares and half a class nodding and scribbling down a note. I stopped and offered a definition that I only barely understood at the time. I said that it seemed to me that a writer's mind has several components, like a cow's four-part ruminant stomach, each to do a separate part of the writing. (Regarding the biologically unsavory nature of this metaphor, I would note that food transforms into energy just as our brain's intake of information transforms into the energy of ideas, similarly without thought.) We exist in a constant sea of internal emotions, settings, relationships, memories, and associations. The most crucial part of the brain, the fifth brain, is the one that synthesizes all these streams of information. These streams make up your imagination and it's up to you to trust that your imagination is singular to you and that if you want to write, you have what you need to do so.

You have your own pattern of mind, created by your imagination and the knowledge you've gathered, and as a writer, it is your work to learn these patterns for your own writing pleasure. You can learn how to access your imagination at any time. You can learn to honor this ability like you would any sacrament, ones you make in marriage or parenting or as a doctor or warrior or activist or otherwise. You can carve out time for your art. You can commit to it.

Some writers are accomplished at blocking the fifth brain: over-intellectualizing, allowing real or imagined editors' harsh critiques, dismissing fresh ideas as not-being-worthy, imagining your failure ahead of time. These struggles result in frustration for the writer. Instead of this fretting, you can trust that it's important to write. You can get out of the way. There's no work to reach the fifth brain. It's already in there. All you have to do is start. Write a sentence about yearning. Write a sentence about something you see when you look up from this book. Write a sentence about one of your internal organs.

When I wrote my first novel, I didn't know to trust my fifth brain. I worked for six months on the last paragraph. I couldn't find the ending. I gnawed on it. I worried it. I wrote version upon version of endings that felt wrong. I was afraid I might never find it. One afternoon I sat down at my desk and a minute or two later I had the ending written. It came to me whole. There was no soaring music, no parade or fanfare, but it was a majestic, thrilling moment in my writing life. It happened so quietly.

Now that I have a relationship with my fifth brain, I know that I needn't have worried. I needed to keep thinking towards the ending, hoping for it, and waiting. My brain was working on it the whole time. You could say it took me the five years of living through writing the book to arrive there or you could say it took the six months of working on the ending or you could say it took the sixty seconds to write the final sentence. All of those are true, and regardless, it was worth the wait.

Writing takes some difficult skills, such as leaning in when you want to back away, confidence in the face of vulnerability, knowing how to experiment and trusting that you won't die before you get a chance to revise. You'll fail and in failing, develop a deeper intimacy with your writing. You can learn to love the writing more than a dream of success for the writing. You can learn that the act of writing is success. You can write a successful word, a sentence, an entire text. You can be proud of any part of your writing. Even one perfectly selected word can be successful. After all, this is all that writing is, one selected word after another. This pride can help you see where you want to take a text.

It can be embarrassing to be proud of something you've written. After all, what if later you decide it isn't any good, or someone else says it isn't any good? That's okay. Love it in the moment. Just as you can't love a friend or partner or a child based on their every action in every moment, you can let love for your writing build over time, in small moments and gestures. Writers must risk that love to finish writing something.

Sometimes writers want equations, acronyms, measurements, things that in other realms would signify our learning or accomplishments. For most of us, writing doesn't work like this. There isn't a list of ingredients, because *we are the ingredients,* and we are always changing. At a biological level, we are shedding cells, firing new synapses, our brains beginning to fray after a certain age. Emotionally and intellectually, we are always growing (and changing). The world around us changes daily, too. The weather, the news, the culture, the moods of those we share our lives with. A deadly virus emerges. Our planet dries or floods or cracks or explodes. The earth circles the sun. We are of this changing matter. Our work, our writing, must change also. How we say things will change. What we have to say will change. We must accept this loose footing of being a writer on the ever-changing soil of our own cells.

Rather than rules or charts or absolutes, you have your own brain. People fall into the trap of believing that there is only one way to write, only one kind of text that is "good," only one way of writing that is successful. There is no one way to write. There is no one way to write at any step of the process of creation. You can do it any way that you desire. You will develop your own right way, and even that will change over time. The most essential tools for being an artist are already inside each artist. Why you write, what you seek to understand, and the shape of your experiences reside always within you.

Writing requires many things: willingness, experimentation, listening, sometimes luck, flexibility, imagination, pacing, humility, bravery, determination, and love. Mostly love. Love for yourself, love for the text you want to share, love for the craft that offers you ways to share it, and love for your reader (if you want one), who is going to gift you hours of their life in the reading. You must grow confidence in your rights as an artist. The most accomplished writers still worry about every new text they begin, but they understand that the only way to really know if it's worth the trouble is to write it.

Feel free to skip around in this book or revisit the same chapter multiple times as needed. Choosing a chapter that draws your interest for any reason is a first exercise in accessing your fifth brain. Some of you will want to begin at the beginning. Some of you might be drawn to the chapter on bending time or art bearing truth. Trusting your instincts is paramount to the work in this book.

In this book I offer some of my stories and craft, things my fifth brain wants me to say about writing, but this book is meant to help you reflect inward, to ask yourself about yourself, as a person of language and understandings. What is it that you have to say? What are your lenses? Your obsessions? Your ghosts? Your dreams? Your vocabularies? What is in your blood and bone and brain? How will you make time? How will you support your writing? The way your imagination is shaped and will spill out is different from the way mine does. Know that it is important that you write, too. I am glad to have your ideas added to the great wealth of things to read. You have something to say, and you can devote the time and love to say it. It is wonderful that you are you, and you can come forward from that specific place and write. Everyone has creative possibility, whether they believe it or not.

Fill your tiny notebooks. Claim some space for your ideas. Go ahead and leave some evidence behind.

Experimenting with Five Brains

In the fifth brain metaphorical paradigm, I propose that there are multiple levels that function in a writer's brain, five kinds of rumination. These brains merely offer a way to conceive of how your imagination works. Which brain we tend to operate from defines our writing style and choices about textual content, but this might change over time. In the infinity of books on the shelves of the world, you will find styles driven by different functions of the brain. This book speaks most often to the fifth brain, which everyone has, and which is a main source of each individual's creativity.

I see the functions of the brain this way: the first brain of the writer is interior/emotional space, how a person feels in any moment. The second brain deals with the external space, the physical, geographical details. The third brain attends to any relational constructs. Is there a person present, are they talking, or are you/the character alone? The fourth brain is associative, pulling from memory and applying these ideas to the moment. The fifth brain makes the connections between all these things, is the meaning-maker.

There is no need to memorize these "functions of the brains." You can use these concepts to develop a sense of what kind of creative animal you are. Or you can use them to look at how to move a scene forward or how to develop a character. Fifth brain work is about learning your own inclination, your own material, your own themes, habits, and rituals. It requires a softening, a rejection of hierarchies where gatekeepers tell you whether you have succeeded or not. It's about loyalty to your own imagination, your own process, to finding how to articulate your view of the world.

Do you feel like writing?

Write a sentence (or more) from each of the five brains. Try using the same moment for each brain. It could be this moment, or one from last week, or a moment from a character's life you've been building, or a moment from an historical event that interests you. Here are the five brains of a writer as I imagine them (all in first-person point of view, for simplicity):

First brain: Interior Space/Emotional (How do I feel right now, inside.)

> *I feel like I'm waiting for something.*

Second Brain: External Space/Physical Details (Where am I?)
> *I am seated in a hard chair in a window-filled room on an island in the Mediterranean, and evening sun brightens the white village buildings across the valley.*

Third Brain: Relationships/Conversation (Who/how am I in relation to other beings around me?)
> *I am alone.*
> Or: *The neighbor's tabby cat is always at the edge of the door, staring in.*

Fourth Brain: The Memory Collector (What do I remember? This is detail, sensory or concrete, and accesses the files of associative memory.)

Fifth Brain: Meaning-Maker/Zone/Mythical Ability/Intuition/ Inspiration/Muse/Love. This is the brain that makes the connections, takes the strings between all the above, develops and pulls from your philosophies, your sensory memory, your relationships, your physical situation, your memory. The fifth brain pulls material from all previous reading and thought.

In Cyprus, seven thousand miles from my home, I realize I have put myself on pause. If I were a machine, it's as though all my wires have been detached and replugged in new places. I don't know what time it is, what is culturally appropriate, what's the right way to spend a day, how much to clean, how much to write, when to turn left or right, when to go get WIFI. Should I wash those towels, how long have I been here, when do I go make friends with the people Mom knows and who said to "stop by anytime"? What should I eat? When should I eat? Did I already eat? Who do I pay the 2.50 Euros for this sun bed? Should I stay at the campground longer? Should I go home? Is it time to go do something brave? I know I did this on purpose, yanked the machine of my life out of its rack. It's like I'm hitting an enormous RESET button, and it's too late to not hit it. I'm already there. I'm in that long minute where I must sit still and let time pass before I restart the thing. It's all dark and I'm waiting, fingers crossed.

(This example is from a letter I was writing to friends when I was alone in Cyprus for five weeks. I didn't know what this paragraph was about when I began writing, but once I wrote the paragraph, it taught me that I was resetting my life after some massive changes had occurred. Fifth brain magic!)

Do you feel like writing?

Let's look at the rich soil of metaphor. I use the cow stomach metaphor to help me describe the fifth brain. The ruminant stomachs have four compartments which have formal and informal names: The rumen (paunch), the reticulum (honeycomb), the omasum (manyplies), the abomasum (true stomach). There's plenty of play to be had in any collection of words. Put *honeycomb*, *paunch*, *manyplies*, and *true stomach* in a page of writing.

Do you feel like writing?

Find something else that has compartments that could be named and used metaphorically. Rooms in a home. Words in a sentence. Parts of a body. Parts of a car. Parts of a painting. Chambers of the human heart. Branches of the government. Parts of a flower. Parts of the eye. Parts of speech. Parts of a microscope. Choose one of these and write a list of the parts. Next, assign the many chambered object a parallel to some other concept you want to write about and let each part speak, or write a memory related to each part.

CHAPTER TWO

Your Material Chooses You

I'm not writing, people complain to me.

I say, *Are you sure?*

It took me a long time to understand that all of life can be writing, too, or can surprise you with ideas you weren't expecting. Giving yourself space and time to pluck images from the surrounding world, allowing new fascinations to emerge is part of writing, but we rarely acknowledge how vital this seeing, this daydreaming, is for the writer. Going to museums, eating french fries in a bar, working a gas pump, listening to a friend lie about her life and letting her do it, reading books, watching movies, petting pets, bitching about the construction across the street, crying over a lost love, writing emails, taking classes, working cash registers, selling insurance, sleeping, eating eggs, recovering from procedures, gardening, playing video games, getting terrible news, freaking out about politics, baking bread, riding a train, suffering a headache, staring at clouds. It can all be writing because so much of writing comes from your lived experiences. I am interested in humans, so all my time with humans is also writing. If you only want to write ecological books, get outside. If you want to write about baseball players, listen to the games in your car, go to them, read up on them. This is writing, too. Writers spend a lot of hours fretting about the time that they aren't writing, but a writer is always writing, always gathering. Something is always cooking in that fifth brain. So much of any artist's life, externally and internally, is intangible. I suggest that we let it all count.

Of course, if you never put anything on the page, or develop it, then you're not producing texts. If you want to make something that someone will read, then you need to sit down and do the writing and print it out or send it out. But might you still be writing in your head, even if you don't print or send? Yes, you might. Is it fine to write for the self alone? Of course it is. What you do with your brilliance is all yours.

Gathering material is different for each person. I went on a camping trip one summer and gathered images that I feel might appear in a text someday. A fairyland of two-hundred-foot pines. My subconscious splashing back at me from canyon walls. Fish, fanning quietly in a lake, seen through binoculars. On their own, these images are a lot of random nothingness. Glimpses of things that caught my eye. These chance images seem like nothing, and they might be nothing in someone else's mind. Inside of me, however, these visions await their stories. Only you can recognize this hum and know when you and the world are agreeing on an idea for a text someday.

In *The Art of Description*, Mark Doty writes, "What descriptions describe is consciousness." You have your own consciousness, utterly specific to you. Your consciousness directs you to these visions. It's helpful to cultivate an awareness of your topics, of what you most often want to describe. What are the conflicts you're interested in, the types of characters, objects, places, reappearing themes? We all have our own subjects. What you notice is meaningful. Who we are is buried in the details of what we notice. Who we are as people, certainly, but also, who we are as writers develops because we allow these details to captivate our attention and to tell us their stories.

As an example, I offer my history with stray cats, who find me every place I live. While I can't adopt all the stray cats that show up, I can think about why stray, homeless, needy things show up for me. What I have in common with them. What we deserve or want. I bet you that I could find a symbolic stray cat, if not a literal one, in every text I've ever written.

I come to these stray cats by no accident, even if you only dig lightly at my past. I was a joint custody child. During my years of custody, my parents moved multiple times around town and every two weeks, I moved from one parent's home to another, wherever it was. As a teenager at night, I snuck out of my parents' homes, crossed neighborhoods effortlessly in the dark to get to friends' houses whose parents were out of town, to drink liquor and watch David Bowie on MTV. Like stray cats, I lived everywhere but nowhere in particular. I know how to move houses and states better than I know how to stay put somewhere. Stray cats might symbolize my struggle to find home. They teach me something about myself and they infiltrate the writing I do.

I suggest that you accept the stray cats that come to you, the material that appears before you, and trust your particularities, the things that mark you as you. Why do they mark you? In *The Art of Mystery*, Maud Casey talks about the "unparaphrasable content in a novel, the experienced meaning." We don't know why you are taken with the things that you are taken with, but they appear, nonetheless. They become the experience. The meaning that you, specifically you, imbue the image with and then must capture. Or perhaps must capture so that you can understand it. It's a nuance, a gesture that we feel we must work with. The images that attract us are not always what we expect them to be, but you can trust that your fifth brain is selecting them for you.

The poet, Arthur Sze, mentions something like Maud Casey's "experienced meaning" in an interview with *Terrain*, saying:

> Last summer I was in Havana, Cuba for a week, for an international poetry festival, and the moment I saw a man pushing this huge cart with dangling onions on the street, it was an unforgettable image. I didn't know what to expect from Cuba. I knew that moment, that image, would find its way into a poem. And it's not like I see something and think I'm going to put that in a poem. It might be years later that I see something and then through recollection, through memory, it comes back.

It's hard to authenticate ourselves as writers. To say to people we're traveling with, *this image matters*, but it's a muscle that we develop, and once it's developed, we will stop everything if we need to, to write down, sketch, and memorize such images.

The symbols you are drawn to might work in various ways to illuminate your life as well as your artistic work. Once I allowed two stray cats to take over my study. I created a pet door with a cardboard frame to the outdoors. Something was happening inside of me, and I needed those strays around. I couldn't have explained it. It was inconvenient. They brought in live lizards, decapitated birds, feathers, a wing with a gristled knob at one end. They left smears of blood on the floor. One morning, I found two little objects on my desk chair: a tiny yellow-beaked baby finch head and a small, dark, licked-clean organ, possibly a gall bladder or kidney.

My manuscripts, in piles around the room, were marked by their footprints, skittered with dirt. The cats mewed happily when they saw me. Sometimes cobwebs hung from their whiskers. They were both tamed and wild. They reminded me of something about myself. I brought civilization, daily, to that room, and then I let the cats wild it again. I let this happen and I unhappened it and it happened and I unhappened it. Since they did not find their grisly work remarkable, I ceased to react to it as well. I merely took the gifts of head and organ off my chair, threw them into the yard, and sat down to write.

The cats reminded me that I can unhinge myself from being so human, with all the niceties, politeness, the adherence to a schedule, the necessary responses to other humans. To be a writer is to be a little hard to tame. The cats commit to their now-hood, their need-hood, their moment-hood. They reminded me to attach to my imagination, my writing, my wilder self. Out of this experience of sharing my space with these two cats came a short story, "The Empty House," a story that surprised me, came out of nowhere, alerted me to a sadness in my life, and basically wrote itself.

I could perseverate over all these obsessions. Why let stray cats into my stories? Why my other subjects? Fairy tales, World War I, a myth of an island. Because I can commit. I am a writer. I have to commit to projects that only exist as inklings in my heart or imagination. I must commit to the dream of a story I haven't written to write it. I must love a story enough to write it, knowing it may never get finished, or published, or read by another. I have devoted my life to stray narrative, ideas, imagination, to loving that which no one else might love. I believe in things that are alive and happening. I practice such love, such allowance, such potentially pointless effort. Like the unpublished works in my study, the cats were vibrant, vital stories that hadn't found homes but were always, already worthy of love.

I've been comforted by a dream that at my funeral, all my characters will be sitting there. And in the front row, every stray cat I've ever loved. These are markers of the life I've lived. I've chosen to accept my subjects, my writing, my style.

A lot of "experienced meaning" occurs in non-situations, non-moments with plain objects of life. I'm not expecting these moments when they appear. I suppose that I look, to others, like a woman staring into space. Early in my writing life, I was sitting in a bookstore cafe on my lunch break, scribbling away in my notebook, and I was startled by a sound, a miniature rustling. I glanced up in time to see a tiny potted purple iris bloom. I heard and saw a flower bloom while I was writing. It seemed symbolic, and I thought it portended great things. I assumed that it was related to my writing because in my writing life at the time, I was moving into my own voice, my own ferocity. After all, wasn't I writing on my lunch break while the others chatted in the break room? Didn't I deserve some sort of sign for the two jobs, plus writing, plus relationship, that I was somehow managing? Here it was, a sign that writing might be light, effortless.

As it turned out, the iris was just on its own timetable. I still had many years before I finished writing a story. I broke up one relationship, started another, moved, joined a writing group, attended grad school, developed my voice and habits, and then, finally, maybe four or five years after that iris bloomed, I had my first story published. Ten more years passed before I published a book. If you weigh the years, weigh the manuscripts, weigh the postage (because once upon a time you had to send everything by mail), weigh the journals upon journals, it wasn't miraculous or effortless or light. In reality, devotion to writing is muscular, determined, heavy work.

I thought, for a while, that the iris was a little liar. It made growing look so poofy and light and delicate. But writing is as lovely as that iris blooming, also. It is. I love making sentences and stories, big or small, more than anything else in the world. It can be as amazing and miraculous as a tiny flower blooming. One of the aspects of being human that shows up in my writing is the capacity to grow. Or how someone doesn't grow and bloom. That iris didn't necessarily portend great things for my writing career, but it did crinkle, rustle, and bloom right in front of me. I saw it and I made a note and now I've given it to you, all these years later.

One summer I was driving through Diné lands, and a dark shape rose in the landscape. It was there for miles and miles, not really getting any bigger, but while I drove, I began to feel a story about a girl trapped up at the top of this mesa, where a massive crow made her solve riddles for her meals. I drove, a modern woman, completely unhindered, traveling alone, the opposite of this girl. I dreamt of her up high in that rock, held hostage for something she'd never done, paying a ransom for a mistake her mother made. Of course, it broke the monotony of driving, but beyond that, it filled me with joy to invent and dream. As soon as I could, I pulled over to a safe spot on the highway and ate my lunch while I dreamed up more of the story, gazing across a field of horses at the vision of the mountain, and gazing at the vision inside of me.

It would have been just as easy not to stop. To not let the joy wash over me. To not indulge myself in this moment of invention. We tend not to, because we're adults and should be "productive," because we have reservations at hotels, or plans, and we're not here to daydream, for heaven's sake. But what is the point of having such a rich, well-fed, encouraged imagination if I'm only going to make it produce something? If I'm only going to chain it to the computer and command it to spin gold? It is vital to let the daydreams roll through, to leave your castles and monsters and inventions alive and free to roam.

It's not always easy to accept the material that our fifth brain offers, especially when that material moves into uncharted areas. It's like an electric shock to witness a writer who is onto something. When it happens to you, or when you see it happen to someone else, it's thrilling. So much of a writing life is the grueling work of research, writing, transcribing notes, being worried about the next step, organizing, fighting writing, fighting not-writing, so that the moment of pleasure at success is priceless and rare. One day over grilled cheeses my writing group discussed new material that E was writing. They were flash fiction pieces about bored metalhead teens making questionable choices. Our group was excited, but it was complex work E was facing. He noted that the experiences he was writing left scars he had to deal with, but also, he said, "Writing about this, in this format, is the easiest writing I've ever done." The material was gritty. E didn't necessarily want to experience it, comb through it again. Writers must endure the sordid wreckage sometimes. You can always choose not to publish something you've written, but in my experience, writers must write the ideas that come because rejecting material can leave you in front of a blank page, chewing your nails or writing social media posts about having writer's block.

I can't tell you how many tables I have leaned over, looked an artist or writer in the eye and said, "You are the only one who can make your art. Do it. I dare you." Some stories are challenging in content, either because we're looking back at people we knew or because we're looking at the present at the people we know or we're looking forward to potential readers who might be colleagues, family, friends. Any of these views can paralyze a story. E had to stay in his seat, in his imagination, and write stories about troubled people he once knew, regardless. It marked a moment in his writing life, and a text that needed tending.

Once I was in a taxicab at a writing conference, and the cabdriver asked the writers in the car what we wrote. One of my friends told him about my story, "Tail," where a woman grows a tail (tale) and must decide whether she is going to live with her strangeness or not. The cabdriver said instantly, "I'd keep it. I'd keep the tail. You have to be what you are." Part of who you are is signified by the material that comes to you.

What I am saying is tend your stray cats. They have come here for you.

Do you feel like writing?
Someone is trapped in the top of a castle, fort, building, house, department store. This person or creature is being guarded by a large creature. Something is being withheld. Someone has been offended, or someone else backed out on a deal. Free the trapped person/creature.

Do you feel like writing?
Find a symbol for what writing looks like in you. Here's mine:

Once I saw an uprooted tree on the bank of the Rappahannock River in Virginia. It was enormous. The underside of its body was a mass of knobs, big as newborns. It was dense with tubers fizzling out into great hairy clumps. There were nodules and sinuous roots re-entering the body of the tree at every juncture from which they did not originate. All of it dripped with mud and sand, an obscenity of growth. When I saw it, I thought, that is what writing looks like in me.

See what symbol comes to mind when you think of writing inside of you. Trust yourself to have an image. If nothing comes up immediately, look for images in the computer, typing in something you are always drawn to: tree, monster, pond, natural disaster, fairy, meadow. You could also go to a library and pull a variety of books with pictures from the shelves and look there. Scroll through images until something hums to you, or feels like you, or looks like you imagine your writing. Carefully write out a description of this thing, noting as many details as possible. Then connect those details to aspects of your writing life. For example, in my uprooted tree image, my fierce desire to write looked like those "great hairy clumps." The fact that any aspect of my living might make it into writing is how I see those "nodule and sinuous roots re-entering the body of the tree at every juncture." The reference to "newborns" symbolizes the abundance of stories that await me.

Make Art for No Particular Reason

Once I watched my friend, M, a brilliant visual artist, as she carved, assembled, and painted a three-foot Dirga statue. As she attached the intricate copper-tipped, detachable arms, M said, "Sometimes I think, *why make that?*"

I was shocked to hear this question. No one thinks like M does. She is a vessel of her art. When she allows her imagination to come forth, when she taps in, wonder follows. The answer to her question was obvious, wasn't it? The shape and the craft and the color and the humor or the sorrow or the majesty of her work, wasn't that always enough? I thought of M's question and answered it, because we need you, and because you need to make it. I told her this and all sorts of other encouraging things that day, but she shrugged.

The reasons we make art are largely intangible.

Months after I'd had this discussion with M, I was on a beach where I found a snail leaving a trail of humped, brightly slimed sand in a lovely line behind it. I took a picture, printed the photo, wrote *Why Make That?* on the back, and sent it to her. The snail's sculpted and slimed sand seemed to answer M's aesthetic question: you make that because you want to, or you need to, or you can't help it. Maybe all those reasons. Maybe just one of those reasons. Maybe it's a choice. Maybe it keeps rising to your conscious mind. Maybe you resist. Maybe you realize what pleasure there is in making a thing that only you can make. Maybe it's time to make it.

I've known M for many years now, and she's never stopped making her wondrous art. Even if she doesn't know the reasons why. The snail and its sand sculpture didn't necessarily convince her, but it taught me that we don't have to know why we make art.

For some, the why-make-that question reveals our attitudes about the usefulness of art. My poet friend, T, wishes that poetry was more tangibly useful. He struggles with the concept that art can do enough practical good in the world, like a bloodmobile, an ambulance, a carpenter. When we have this discussion, I am always fervent. *The Brothers Karamazov* changed my ideas on religion. *Roots* burned the irreconcilable human failure of slavery into me. *Jane Eyre* taught me that there are consequences. *Beloved* taught me about the impossibilities of love. *Autobiography of Red* taught me a new capacity for tenderness. *The Wind-Up Bird Chronicle* pushed me forward into my imagination. Writers have these lists, books that altered or illuminated their brains. Through reading, I've traveled the world, traveled through time. Difficulties in my life are often directly addressed in poems or stories or novels or essays. *Oh,* I think when I read, *that's how I can handle that* or I think, *Well, that is not the way I'd do that.* I know that people are behind these written texts, people like me, sorting out their human lives, in other times, in other worlds, and their experiences and craft lift me from the leaden gravity of this body and this life. They lend their fresh paths and choices and suggestions without even knowing I'm out here, needing them. That is some genuine good in the world.

That's why.

A prose writer, K, had an essay about her miscarriage published in a fine literary magazine, but she called me, crying, saying, "Why did I write that? Why did I publish that? Now I must experience it all over again. I'll have to suffer it all again!" I assured her that there were readers who needed the work, who needed her honest story, just as it was. By that evening, many women who had suffered similar agonies wrote her to say how much courage it gave them to read her story, how it made them want to speak of their own sorrow. Her honesty lent them space for their own grief.

That's why.

Another prose writer pal, E, hates sitting at the computer. He'd rather be doing almost anything outside, active, physical, visual, but he forces himself because stories come to him, and he must write them down. It goes against the grain of who he is otherwise, but he submits to the stories. He can't help it. They belong to him.

That's why.

We make art because there is something in us that we must say and there is an art form through which we can articulate it. We say it for ourselves, and we say it for the people who need to hear it. We say it for people who might not have their own art form, their own clarity, through which to express it. We say it for people who don't even know what they need to hear. We say it because we must.

Sometimes writing is like following something you can't really see as it heads right into your own marrow. Ursula Leguin, in *Steering the Craft*, writes, "To make something well is to give ourselves to it, to seek wholeness, to follow spirit. To learn to make something well can take your whole life. It's worth it." This brings us back to the question of *why make that?* Even though her book is generally about the tools of writing, Leguin reminds us that writing in earnest is a matter of wholeness, spirit, a matter of making your life meaningful.

For years I pored over two books with brief biographies and photographs about writers to answer this question about why I write. These books were *The Writer's Desk*, a book of photographs by Jill Krementz, and *The A-Z of Great Writers* by Tom Payne. Once during a conversation, I pulled out *The A-Z* to reference Euripides or Muriel Spark or Anna Akhmatova and my friend, H, said, "Oh! You actually read that. I kind of thought it was just a prop, like a doorstop or something." It is a large and unattractive book, but I remember how I felt when I first opened it and saw a slew of notes about the lives and work of writers over centuries. I found my lineage there (even though these are not, certainly, the only great writers in the world). It was a remaindered book, so I could afford it, too, which was a significant win at the time.

The Writer's Desk is focused on more modern American writers in their own writing spaces and includes electric typewriters and laptops (modern for 1996!). There's Amy Tan using a laptop with her little dog nearby and there's Rita Dove at a standing desk with lit candles. I saw into the privacy of these writing rooms and human stories and knew that they were like me, regular people who also saw something in their imaginations that they wanted to translate for others on the page.

Why do I make stories? Because narrative (storytelling) is my most essential obsession. I am curious about the eternal samenesses, the archetypes, and archetypal situations, in human life throughout time. I think that the word "narrative" could be replaced with the word "soul." The soul is a metaphor for who we are in essence. These essences might be known by the narratives of our lives. A child is born. The story of the birth begins her. (Begins her, him, they, *someone*.) The story of her parents/adopted parents/or lack of parents shapes her. Her siblings/or no siblings and friends shape her. The story of her DNA shapes her. The story of her feeding patterns, sleeping patterns, of the world at the time when she's born, all of this becomes part of her narrative. Her abilities and disabilities shape her. How she is treated for the color of her skin shapes her. How her body is built and how she perceives it shapes her. The essence of a person grows and grows and grows with each experience lived and told.

You create a story about who you are, all the varieties of who you are, and how you move through those varieties, until you die. And for a while after, other people tell those stories of you. And you live life and tell your stories from within this narrative soul, from your perspective, from this story that you are.

This is my subject, then. Human narrative, human soul, the great human story. This human story goes on and on. Individually, we eventually stop. Drop dead, or lose our minds, or fall out of memory. But the story does not end. Not yet. All apocalypse books imagine the story going on *after* the apocalypse. We can't even imagine the end of the world without more story.

That means there's room for you to write.

Go ahead and make it, whatever it is. From this perch of aliveness, from the narrative story of you, maybe you simply answer the why-make-that question with *because*.

Do you feel like writing?

Get comfortable somewhere to write, public or private. Bring stuff to write. Look at this stuff and think about it. What do you need? What do you write with? Do you use your hands? Note the scars, spots, jewelry, palmistry, fingernails, state of disrepair or care, coloring, size of the wrists, history of injuries, things you use the hands for the most (typing, cutting food, clicking light switches, caressing skin, inserting keys, holding brooms). Do you type your thoughts? Do you speak into a machine? Describe the computer or keyboard or another device. Is it pristine? Is it marked up? Are there stickers on it? Does it have a texture? Is it clean or dirty? What kinds of communication do you use it for? If you don't write or use a machine, do you dictate to a human? Describe the organization of this, how often your transcriber arrives, what days, how your system of communication works. There are stories embedded in any of these details. Find them.

Do you feel like writing?

Perform a *Why Make That* inquiry: Who is your writing for? When did you first want to write? What drives your writing? What do you hope will happen for your reader?

Do you feel like writing?

Name a character after yourself and put them in a scene where you wouldn't know what to do. See what this version of you does.

CHAPTER FOUR

Bend Time

Every writer I've ever known has said at some point, *I just want time to write.*

This is what I know about making time in the writing life: you must be dogged, and you must be fluid. What is fluidity for writers? It is the possibility of making the impossibility-of-no-time into writing time. If you are a writer feeling like you're not a writer because you have no time, because you have no money, because your faith is lapsing, because your good work isn't recognized, remember this: the river of writing is always inside of you. It belongs to you. It is ever present. Sometimes it's murky green and filled with bloated cows. Sometimes it sparkles and slaps with fat leaping fish. Other times, it is only a watery thread in black muck. Regardless of its incarnation, it is always there. It is your fifth brain, and it belongs to you and only you, and you are responsible for it.

The river will always be there. What you need to focus on is your path to the river. Your method of returning. Will you not venture down if there are brambles or poison ivy or hidden beasties? Will you try new paths any time you have to? Will you do it because you love it? This might look like writing at a certain time every day or week. Or writing a sentence or line every day. Or writing three pages a day or once a week. It doesn't matter what writing looks like for you if you find a way to make writing fit into your days if you want it to. These are paths to the writing river that you are tamping down, cutting back, paving with stone so that in this busy life, you can skip down there quickly when you have a minute.

I have suggestions for making the time in your days more fluid. For most of my working life, I've chosen to spend my lunch breaks or dinner breaks writing. One of the things I have learned in this lifetime of work breaks is how to make the time work for me. How to make this time into a moment of imagination or language or something other than the paid work you've been doing. I find a place to sit and be with my own mind, maybe a coffeeshop, a bench, a park, a library, a car.

It would be just as easy to say to myself, I am already working a job, I will write when I have more time, but I have kept at the writing, always, no matter what because it matters to me. I have trained myself to get the writing done through a thousand lunches. If I can't write, I watch YouTube videos that relate to whatever I'm writing, or to the subject of writing. Or I eat with a colleague who writes. I find ways in that hour to connect to my writing life because I know it's vital to my overall balance. And I write when I can. If I can't, I wink at it from afar, assuring it that I will be back when I can. Maybe I write in the mornings before work, in the evenings, on the weekends. I learned how to fill in the cracks with what is salient to me. Writing has never earned me much money, so if I wanted it, I had to figure out a way to do it without anyone else caring that I did it. I must consistently honor the fact that writing is an essential love of mine.

Creating this fluid-time requires some invention. In the nineties, I worked in a bookstore in Charlotte, NC as a clerk, and at night, I had a two-hour break before I went back and became the cleaning crew for the store. During this break, I ate dinner from a Tupperware as I crossed a plaza to the library. Then I took up a spot in the library, spread out my notebook, wrote a few sentences, did a writing exercise, or looked something up. It was blissful, but soon it was time to go back to the store and clean. Before I left the library, I would choose an image or atmosphere from my writing to savor while I cleaned. Back at the store in the mop closet, I pulled the yellow bucket under the big faucet and let the water gush while I thought about the image. I imagined it from different senses, from different directions. I fleshed it out. The water poured; the yellow bucket filled. Sometimes, because I didn't have pen and paper, I would write a few words with my finger on my leg, so that I could have a memory of the new information when I got back to the page. You can invent ways to keep your writing life alive for you. It can be so tiny, so invisible to others. But you will know.

Another ritual involves paying deep attention, even if you are ringing up customers or buying stocks or serving food or selling real estate or teaching a class. Events in these places can bring you a story, a character, an instance, a mood, a line, a moment. Maybe someone says something in a conversation. Maybe there's a line in a movie. Maybe you get an idea while you're driving. Always scratch it down somewhere, someway. This is writing, being attuned and fluid. Look at these notes later and see where they fit. Your fifth brain is always working for you, and it can remember what you are working on, no matter where you are, especially if you've been visiting the work sometimes, taking the path down to the river.

Once in the Philadelphia Art Museum I was looking at a thick yellow triangle in one of Van Gogh's sunflower paintings and suddenly, a portal in my imagination opened. I could see a small room with a dirty floor. There was an old rind of cheese on a wooden table, and I could hear someone murmuring and moving around in a corner of the room out of sight. This felt like an idea for a story and without really thinking about it, since I didn't have a pen, I used a finger to trace a few words on my thigh again and again, "triangle," "wooden floor," "cheese," so that I could remember to explore it in writing later.

The friend I was with noticed my hand on my leg and asked what I was doing. "I guess I'm writing," I replied. A look of surprise crossed my friend's face.

She asked me, "Are you always writing?"

I said, "Maybe," and then I shrugged and added, "probably." I had been writing for a few years when this happened, and I knew from experience that if I didn't write down an idea that I'd lose it, even if it wasn't in ink. I didn't know yet that I was always writing, always seeking, gathering, and sifting ideas. I didn't understand that I'd given myself permission to do this, to be a writer in any situation anywhere, and that I needed no other permission. I didn't know that my fifth brain was always writing even when I wasn't doing it consciously.

At one particularly toxic job, when others gathered in the break room to discuss our boss' daily manias, I took my sandwich and my notebook to a church around the corner. I sat on a splintery bench in a boxwood hedge and bent my head over my notebook. I wrote one chunk at a time. A few sentences, a paragraph, a few paragraphs. In months, it would be something, but the real magic here was the power those lunches gave me. When I returned to the hysteria of peers and ridiculous instructions from the boss, I was floating. I was 1,000 miles above that store, or below that store. I was elsewhere, immersed in the privacy of my imagination. I was a writer, writing.

I haven't prioritized owning things and I wasn't raising children, so I've had some flexibility in choosing how to make my living. As a result, I have had, at last count, forty jobs. Besides writing. Because of my ferocity about writing, I spent years refusing promotion, insisting on strange hours and manners of employ, skirting careers that didn't make room for writing. This has marked me in many ways. I still refuse certain ambitious steps that my career could take, because I know that I don't want to pretend to care about things I don't care about. Being a writer has made me fierce about living my life meaningfully. It takes an effort to be out of step with America's capitalist culture. There are all sort of ways to live your life and as an artistic person you should think about how you spend your days. I have made choices because I have a sort of mono-vision: most of the time, what I want is time to write.

Because of my devotional practices around writing, writing blooms outward from me. When I finished grad school for an MFA, the New Jersey and Philadelphia colleges where I taught English as an adjunct paid so little that I had to work in a coffee shop, too, to make my rent. I had not been at this coffee shop long, making lattes between grading essays, before people were hanging over the counter asking for prompts, pressing their journals across to me, telling me about the book they would someday write. My writing self has a big aura because I bring my art everywhere I go, in everything I do. Taking inventory in basement bookstores, serving champagne from silver trays, editing books on foot disease, digging ditches, teaching, I am in touch with my fifth brain. This feels like an accomplishment, no matter how intangible. If I died tomorrow, I would know that I spent as much time as possible doing the thing that I love the most.

Often, I am asked about "writer's block." It's possible that writer's block is always something else. Writer's exhaustion, writer-in-love, writer-in-grief, writer-in-trauma, writer-raising-kids, writer-in-transition, writer-in-illness, writer-overwhelmed, writer-embroiled-in-crappy-relationships, writer-making-money, writer-traveling, writer-afraid-of-writing-the-story-that-insists-on-being-written, writer-cringing, writer-thinking. Some of writer's block is probably thinking. Some of it living. Some of it suffering. Some of it reading, some of it learning. Pauses are fine. Month-long, season-long, year-long pauses, many-years-long pauses. Pausing might be painful. But it doesn't have to become grief. It doesn't have to be a loss. A writer can write whenever they want. Of course, I have seen people give it up for years, or give it up for good. These are available choices. But if you need a pause for any reason, take one. Then you can return to writing if you want. You can always return. This is yours. If you love it, you can get back to it. Maybe you can love writing from afar when you can't write and call it reading or thinking. You can always welcome it back. It's as simple as picking up a pen or opening a document. I mean that. Literally, you can return to the relationship this very second. Write a sentence about your current setting, interior monologue, or current problems. Just one line and there you are, writing again.

If you are serious about writing, you know that a casual desire won't result in the act of writing a text. In *Negotiations with the Dead*, Margaret Atwood draws a stark comparison between people who "have a book in them" and dedicated writers, saying, "Or to put it in a more sinister way, everyone can dig a hole in a cemetery, but not everyone is a grave digger. The latter takes a good deal more stamina and persistence. It is also, because of the nature of the activity, a deeply symbolic role." A working writer is a formidable force. They are creating worlds out of their particular imaginations, translating what they see into the abstract concepts of black and white in the form of alphabets and sentences on the page, and while they construct, they consider larger concerns of structure, flow, tense, point of view, and voice. If you are a writer, you know how deep the grave must be dug. How the dirt seeps and refills and must be dug again, and deeper. There might be ghosts, there will be mourners, and loss is inevitable. It is not casual work, and while anyone can try to do it, not everyone will be able to endure it. You must choose how much it means to you and if it means enough to you to bear the highs and lows.

For years at the beginning of every summer when I was teaching full time, I read *Daily Rituals: How Artists Work*, by Mason Currey, to help adjust my sense of fluidity from teaching a full class load to my own writing rhythms. In this wonderful book, Currey has gathered the working methods of writers, artists, musicians, scientists, and philosophers for our review. Samuel Beckett ate scrambled eggs, locked himself in a room for as long as he could stand, then went walking in Montparnasse, drinking red wine and socializing. Maya Angelou got a "mean hotel room" and worked from seven am until two pm. Then she would go home and read and make her hubby dinner. After

Victor Hugo wrote, he'd go on the roof and bathe so that his mistress down the street could see him. Richard Wright wrote in Fort Greene Park, every day, regardless of the weather. One writer stayed in bed all day. Their other hours, non-creative hours, all these people lived lives, worked other jobs, raised kids, wrote letters, made calls, met with lovers, drank, did drugs, took walks. It comforts me to see the passages of their days, the infinite variety of ways to live this life as an artist. We are all making choices.

Time is almost always against writers, because not only do we need it to think, to live, to scribble, to edit, to submit, to revise, to weep, to revise, to get practice, to take classes or join groups, but we also need time for certain texts to develop inside of us. And sometimes we need *years*. We pretend this isn't so. We talk about famous people who wrote books without revising in a brief matter of time, but we don't talk about how rare this is. And when years start piling up, we tend to lie about it. Why? Because non-writers don't understand how long it takes. And who can blame them? The writing demands change with each text. Sometimes I can draft a story in three days and polish it in a month or so. Sometimes a writing problem is resolved in a matter of two minutes of thinking. Sometimes the text quiets and gets left behind. I went to a conference panel on The Ten-Year-Novel once, and there was weeping among the audience. Imagine ten, fifteen years working on a project, and no one really knows except your friends and family! The heart of your life growing stale on paper or in a digital file in a room in your home. It takes courage and fluidity to keep a project going in the face of time.

As a long-term writer, you need to be dogged, and you should probably write for several reasons rather than just one.

Maybe you write to grow your own psychic innards, your own wisdom, your own sense of self in the world. Maybe you write to share the living you've done, to teach us what you have seen. Maybe you write to understand what you've seen and experienced in this world better for yourself. For a long-term writer, reasons beyond publication are imperative. This work can illuminate our lives, illuminate our readers. If we know some of the reasons we are offering this gift to the world, then we can make time for it.

One summer, I looked up and realized I'd written a collection of short fiction over the previous year. While grieving a divorce, teaching classes, laid out by back problems, suffering a bout of shingles, three respiratory infections, and two house burglaries, I was writing a book and I didn't even realize it. Seemingly behind my own back, the stories formed. All of them ended up being fairytales for disappointed women. I wrote my way through the worst year of my life. A book happened anyhow. Despite the demands of living, I had trained myself to write through anything and I did it. You can do it. It can be done.

You can dream the writing life, invent the writing life, demand the writing life. Bending time is about transforming the world into your writing room.

Do you feel like writing?

Write a list of times, places, and people who make you feel the most like your writer self. This is a simple exercise but naming what gets us to the river of writing is a way to identify what we need more of in life. If you don't have any friends to talk to about writing, then maybe you need some. If you haven't ever researched your favorite author, go see if there are articles or interviews about that person. Let yourself be inspired by them. Where do you like to write? Can you be in that place more often? If being outside always give you new ideas, go outside. If watching foreign movies, listening to hip hop, or reading poetry always ends up with you scratching out a new idea, go do those things.

Do you feel like writing?

Imagine how to fit some new rituals for writing into the schedule you have in your life right now. Not someday, but today. Can you make ten minutes? Write one sentence? Write one word?

CHAPTER FIVE

Pay Attention to
Your Knowledge Banks

Our lives develop into specific sets of experiences, studies, curiosities. Each of us creates an individualized set of habits and knowledge banks. Are you versed in NYC streets or banking or Japanese recipes or street smarts or riding horses or rap musicians or trucking routes or yoga or calculus or fly fishing or harvest ants? Whatever your knowledge banks are, they bear vocabularies that mark you specifically and represent the wealth of your brain. Paying attention to our own history, our knowledge banks, and our embodied vocabularies can be a place to begin writing.

Take your lexicon of memories as an example. As adults, many of our actions are influenced by what has come before. Staying aware that our memories shift, as do our perceptions of the past, we can play with this lexicon any time. Here is an example of how an object can conjure up memories. When I pack for a camping trip, each piece of gear I touch flashes images from previous trips.

I pack my tent and remember being nineteen with my friends in a massive military-style tent in some Maryland woods, watching a skunk roll around in a can full of bacon grease in the middle of the night. It was our first lesson in skunks and bacon grease. *Sorry*, we whispered through the screen tent window, *sorry*.

I pack the cast iron frying pan, remembering a night in Cave Creek, AZ standing over the campfire with an ex, cooking potatoes in that frying pan, even though it was clear that my partner wished he was somewhere else.

I pack my thirty-year-old sleeping bag, remembering the time I camped for a week at the ocean and when I returned a little wild-eyed and wild-haired, a work colleague called me the Wild Man of Borneo. After she said this, I remember flashing a grin at myself in the bathroom mirror, thinking, *finally*.

Each one of these memories could be developed into a text. We can transform them. I can revise the outcomes of any of these moments. I can turn the images into whatever I want them to be. I can turn that tent into a house. I can turn that skunk into a dinosaur. When I transform these memories into stories, I move them into my texts, and I own those stories in new ways. Only then can I understand the symbolism, the things they tell me about life, myself, others, the nature of existence.

Think about how specific each of these experiences is for each person: your first death, a close relative's face, summer in a setting you knew when you were young, losing your virginity, a memorable meal, and so on. These are the knowledge banks of your experience. You might use these stories to write poetry or non-fiction or own your images in drawing or music. It doesn't matter how you transform and own these things, only that you know you have the power to do it. Let yourself freewrite into the ideas that arise. My real life falls apart or blooms again and again and I take its lessons into me, churn them into stories, let them be understood, transformed, made universal. You can rise out of the ordinary hours of your daily life, shiver loose the little ropes of memory or shame, and cast the story in new stones. You can grow orangutans or skyscrapers; you can spin anything anew and there you will find your readers, saying, *yes, yes, I've known this, too.*

After sharing a story set in Paris where I once honeymooned, my friend S asked me how long after the experience I had written the story. Sixteen years, I told her. She commented on how alive my psychogeography is. I had to look up the term. It was invented in the late 1950s in Europe, attributed to Guy DeBord. All the landscapes and places I've spent time in are distinctively alive places in my writing. It doesn't matter if I haven't been there in ten, twenty, or thirty years. I might still write something from a place years later because it is embedded in my psychogeography. The idea points towards the idea of drifting through a setting and letting it heighten your senses, whether consciously and unconsciously. I had an experience in Paris and thought about it for sixteen years. Then I wrote a short story about it, and it was as if no time had passed. I could write about those places in Paris as if I was transcribing images I was seeing that very moment.

The settings we've spent time in become part of our knowledge banks, especially if some experience there was heightened emotionally, or if you paid attention. Every home you've lived in, every town, every grocery store, every place that imprinted itself on you for whatever reason is yours for reinventing. Each of us has a set of psychogeographic locations in our history to explore.

One of my favorite knowledge banks, and one we all have in common, is food. Individually, what we eat and how we eat creates a specific knowledge bank that marks our lives. I always ask people what they've had for lunch, and often they hesitate, as if lunch will reveal something private about them. It does, in fact, but not in any direct way. People often eat dinners together, the same thing for everyone, but often lunches are pretty individual affairs. I can think about what people eat for lunches and extrapolate from there. It's not about judging others; it's about worldbuilding. It's thinking about who is eating what and why.

Sometimes I use lunches as an icebreaker for a class or a gathering. In a class once, a man paused, embarrassed, before confessing that he'd "only" had a granola bar. Who was he imagining would shame him for this? A mother who thought he should eat more? Cultural pressure that says we should have mid-day meals? People are opinionated about food and those opinions are a source of material.

I have one friend who wishes there were a pill for meals because he's tired of bothering. Another friend eats salads made every day by her retired husband. Another friend drinks a premade smoothie from a plastic bottle. In Cyprus, the whole family comes home for lunch at one o'clock, for a big, heavy, freshly prepared meal. In Japan, there might be a bento box. In Nigeria, maybe palm nut soup. These are choices that come from desires or necessities or beliefs or culture or geography or money or attitude. I don't make assumptions about what the choices mean for my friends and colleagues and family, though I do see some symbols there. I enjoy thinking about the ways in which the act of eating shapes or illustrates aspects of our lives and offers vocabularies specific to the eaters.

There are matters of comfort, matters of ease, matters of unease, matters of stuck-ness embedded in lunch vocabularies. I know someone who ate the same turkey sandwich every day for weeks, then for months, then for years: whole wheat bread, green leaf lettuce, a slice of cheese, two slices of turkey. A young teenager I knew twenty years ago never ate lunch at home. She preferred food from restaurants. She either wanted the House Lo Mein with shrimp and chicken and beef from the Chinese place, or an egg salad sandwich at the neighborhood sandwich shop. I knew a young man who ate nothing but salted, plain burgers and french fries. One lunch time I watched a college student spoon a whole avocado into her mouth and wash down bites with swigs of water from a plastic gallon jug. I worked construction with a man who ate two chili dogs and a Big Gulp from 7-11 for breakfast every single day. Each of these rich and unique habitual meals begs for their full stories. This is a font of material.

I'm also interested in when people eat their lunches. Are they early lunchers or late lunchers? Is there wine or water or soda or tea or beer or kombucha or coffee? Does a person eat at 11:00 am, noon, 2:00 pm, not at all? Where are they? Standing at a counter? Sitting at a desk? On a blanket? At a table alone? At a table with colleagues or family? Meals and times and companions are all part of a personal food lexicon.

We're opinionated about food choices and times. It's interesting to investigate how people form these opinions. I was raised to eat dinner with the family no matter what, and so I still set the table for dinner, even though I live alone and am cooking for myself. It's a privilege to have food, to cook food, to eat food. I like to be aware of my luck. In my life of lovers, I was able to study a lot of family meal dynamics. One family gathered around a big table full of take-out bins carefully ordered to each person's taste, although the family spent the whole meal exchanging bitter jabs. Another family gathered around big platters of traditionally prepared food that everyone was sentimental about and excited to eat, but it was only a matter of time until there was a fight, followed by someone weeping. In contrast, one family I knew joyously ordered three boxes of pizza for dinner, and at different times, family members wandered into the kitchen and ate slices for dinner, then breakfast, then lunch the next day.

In the opening of Haruki Murakami's book, *The Wind-up Bird Chronicle*, the narrator is boiling spaghetti when the phone rings and a mysterious woman speaks to him as if he knows her. At one point the narrator says, "'Sorry, but you caught me in the middle of making spaghetti. Can I ask you to call back later?'

The mysterious woman says, 'Spaghetti? What are you doing cooking spaghetti at ten-thirty in the morning?'

'That's none of your business, I said, 'I decide what I eat and when I eat it.'"

The narrator doesn't know the caller or why she's calling and yet she asks this judgmental, intrusive question about what time he's eating a certain meal. As if there is a standard. As if anyone gets a say about what and when you eat. As if their choices are the only choices.

People do decide what they eat and when they eat it, and that is what is so interesting. It is a mistake to think that people perceive meals the same way. Once I watched a Greek man smoke five cigarettes with his sugary morning coffee while he told me that it wasn't healthy to eat breakfast. My shock at this illuminated that I was raised to believe that breakfast was the "most essential meal" (probably from 1970s American television commercials). So much rich material is buried in our eating.

Fictional food can work as prophecy, too. In Margaret Atwood's *Maddadam* series, there are details of what characters eat in the pre- and post-apocalyptic world. Atwood slightly reimagines foods that we eat to show us how close our world is to the apocalyptic reality she's writing. People are addicted to a certain coffee chain, they love buckets of genetically modified fried chicken, they eat energy bars. While I was reading this book, I heard an article about genetically modified chickens on NPR that so closely resembled her fictional food that I forgot that I was listening to the news for a moment. Because I could see food trends from my culture in her apocalyptic fiction, it made me come to terms with the fact that tragic paradigm shifts happen. For example, her fictional implication that a pandemic that can kill millions of people across the globe, shut down commerce, and set off a new chain of previously unimaginable events has been proven to be regrettably real.

Also specific to each of us is our own experience with intimacy. The first crush, kiss, sex experience. The first swoon. The second time you fall in love. The fifth. Or if intimacy for you never looks like what it looks like for others, it still belongs to you. Maybe you've had a string of lovers or no lovers. Or maybe you have dating app stories. Or stories from bed. Maybe there's polyamory. Maybe there are stories of arguments in the car. Old high school flames who find each other in their seventies. There are stories upon stories accrued and connected inside of us like a mess of hyperlinks that we can follow into narrative.

My first kiss was with R, who died in his forties. He tasted like cola, and the memory is twined with the white rug we were on, the legs of the couch near our heads. I remember both of us concentrating on the kissing. We were astonished by the softness of mouths, by the danger of his braces. We both loved it, and that was something we agreed on without speaking of it. Both of our teen lives were messes, but we had this one shared delight. Years later, in our thirties, R was suffering, and he called me to tell me about a band. We hadn't spoken in twenty years. I was walking to the community pool when he called. I sat on a bench and listened to this unwell stranger/not stranger pour out his impassioned thoughts about this music. Was this what we had in common? Our willingness to be impassioned? Or was it the firstness of our love that connected us? Regardless, he's in my history now. He's part of my knowledge banks, a rich and varied source unique to my being and easily accessed by my fifth brain.

Our personal curiosities add to our knowledge banks, too. Some of us went to school to learn more about certain subjects, some of us taught ourselves. Translation, pharmaceuticals, engines, foreign languages, musical notation, mathematics, cybersecurity, sonography, stocks, accounting, nursing, politics, economics, philosophy, poetry, tech, social work, military maneuvers, football, cultures, Greek myths, organisms, and so on. If you studied it, thought about it, learned about it, it's part of you. It inhabits a fold in your brain. Your knowledge banks belong to you. You might think they are uninteresting (because you are accustomed to them) but they *are* you.

What if you thought about these knowledge banks as the specific vocabulary of your existence? Everything that you are can be something that you write about. You can pull from this vocabulary and give elements to characters or poems or let them direct an essay.

Here's a way to use these knowledge banks. Let's take the subject of food again (always a favorite of mine). Are you a person who eats because we're animals that need the energy? Or are you a sensualist who eats because it is a pleasure? How does your character view food? There are portraits awaiting you.

Here is a portrait of a marriage failing, revealed in separate eating: The husband is a cook who loves to try things and makes a different dinner every night. The wife starts asking nights off from dinner, chugging down a vanilla-flavored protein powder mixed with milk instead.

Here is a portrait of aging and losing senses: An elderly woman looks around the busy restaurant and puts a salt and pepper shrimp into her mouth. She asks her granddaughter across the table, "What does it taste like?"

Here is a portrait of camaraderie: Two women order fried chicken sandwiches with pickles and coleslaw and hot sauce and sit at an iron table. The older woman describes a recent awkward one-night stand, and they cackle with laughter, fingers dripping.

In the television show, *Six Feet Under*, the show begins with someone dying. The death I remember most vividly is a single woman getting home from work, microwaving a frozen meal, forking a hunk of chicken into her mouth, and choking on it. She is alone, so her choking cannot be stopped. Her chair falls over and dumps her on the floor. She's eating a lousy frozen meal when she dies. The writers made this choice, and it adds to the pathos of the scene. Why didn't the writers give her a pork chop seared with lemon and garlic, served with an arugula salad and baguette with butter? Because it's even sadder that she's eating such crappy food when she dies.

Here's a portrait of loneliness: Alone in her beige apartment, a single woman chokes on her frozen, microwaved meal and dies.

Where have you been? Who was with you? Whatever the answers to these questions, your fifth brain was present, too. Start writing and see what gems it gathered for you.

Do you feel like writing?

Write down what you had for lunch. Today or yesterday's lunch. Describe the ingredients in detail, where the lunch took place, about the ingredients or the atmosphere or the conversation or the silence. Describe the plates you ate from, the associations you have with those plates, the silverware. Did a server bring you lunch or your best friend or did you make it? Play with associations and symbols and see what stories are embedded in your meals.

Go further. What does one of your parents eat for lunch? Your partner? Your friend? Your sister? Your colleague? Your child? Do you think any aspect of their personality or any symbolism about their lives is revealed in those choices? (Although people can be judgmental about food, resist judgment. Observe lightly.)

Do you feel like writing?

To gain a sense of the scope of your own knowledge banks, play with this exercise on the following page and see how much you know. (Obviously, the list of topics could go on infinitely, and that's the point!)

Examine your knowledge banks and apply the following prompts to the list of one-word topics below the prompts.

- Think of the most immediate memory.
- Think of the most frustrating memory.
- Ask yourself what you still don't know about the topic.
- Ask yourself what you love or hate about the topic.
- Make a list of words associated with the topic.

Random Topics:

- Lunch
- Instruments
- Partying
- Culture
- Eyes
- Injuries
- Arguments
- Writing
- Birds of the Southwest
- Planets
- Philosophy
- Jobs
- Travel
- Family
- Housing
- Place
- Science
- Museums
- Gardening
- French sauces
- Hindi
- Tadpoles
- Mathematics

Once you have messed around in your memories and gained a sense of your vast knowledge banks, find the one that interests you most, has the most heat, or the one that bothers you the most. Create from there.

CHAPTER SIX

Getting Lost

Being lost is a state of not-knowing. We pass in and out of this state throughout our lives, and during the creation of any text. It can be uncomfortable, non-linear, unpredictable, and frightening. Learning to be comfortable in moments of transition and figuring out how to access your fifth brain anywhere are ways of managing lostness.

Once I got lost (literally) in a way that marked a turning point in my writing life (conceptually). I was in my early 20s, and I started to feel alien in my world. I lived in a city that didn't feel right. My boyfriend and I lived in a faux-wood apartment complex, and we worked jobs that seemed like they *might* have to do with our future careers. Our friends were going to have a baby, so we all talked about that. Other friends wanted to buy a house; we talked about that. We talked about higher paying jobs, saving money, buying houses, all of which were things I felt I should want, being in my 20s. But I didn't want them. What I wanted didn't show up in the conversations that I had with my friends.

At the time, I was trying to be a writer. I worked at a bookstore because the job placed me closer to the books I wanted to create, but really, I was in retail, ringing up purchases and writing poems on receipts, participating in meetings about overhead and inventory. My role in this retail life always seemed off to me. One night after work, I accidentally boarded the wrong bus home. When I realized, my heart filled with joy. I was on the wrong bus! I could have stood and rung the bell and walked back down the long driveway to start my journey over on the right bus, but I wanted to stay and see what would happen. It felt like finally, something was happening. I beamed at my fellow passengers and thought, *Let's get fucking lost*. I got out my notebook. We drove into the heart of the city, where I'd only been once or twice. I scribbled descriptions. I made up narratives about the other riders. People got on and off the bus. We drove all the way through the city and into the outskirts, into neighborhoods I didn't recognize. I stared out the window at other people's houses and wondered what they ate for dinner.

It was an uncanny trip. All of us passengers were thrown off the bus at one point, and we stood around in the middle of a neighborhood until the next bus picked us up. It got dark while I rode this second bus. Then the second bus broke down. All the passengers sat in the dark. I could barely contain my pleasure and I scribbled feverishly. How had it come to this? I had no idea where I was. I was alone! I could be this alone! The world could be this big and busy and I could vanish. And I would write. Be anywhere and write!

That strange night, in the darkness of the second broken-down bus, I broke, too. I broke from the wrong life. I broke from expectations and assumptions. I broke from the knowledge of how things were. A third bus picked us up and dropped me back on the very same square of sidewalk I'd departed from hours earlier.

For the next couple of days, I wrote incessantly. I filled notebooks with emphatic, clear, feverish pages of text, and I read. In Robert Boswell's novel, *Geography of Desire*, a wonderful storyteller, Ramon, stares at a spark of light on water and decides he must give up storytelling. In the beige-carpeted bedroom of that apartment complex, that spark of light flew straight through the pages of the book into me. Through ink and paper, through a space-time continuum of one writer's imagination to another, it hit me like a bus. I wasn't just *trying* to be a writer, I *was* a writer, and I simply wasn't living the right life. I didn't want, like other people wanted, babies and a house and a job and security. I believed in being rapt, absorbed, no longer visible, getting on wrong buses, hearing stories, telling stories. I wanted to accept the darkness, the strangers, the unfa-miliar city streets. Getting lost, it turned out, was part of the sacred fabric of my life.

After that bus trip, I decided that I would get comfortable with being lost. I would anchor my life not to the security of tradition, but rather, to the making of narrative. I would have jobs, but I would know they weren't the only thing that mattered. I would translate the world into stories and be found. This revelation forever connected acts of being lost to acts of writing for me, knowing that lostness could indicate an entrance.

I'm not the only one to note the connection between getting lost and narrative. In her book, *The Art of Mystery*, Maud

Casey claims that "[s]tories are how we stand in the presence of mystery." Being lost, literally or metaphorically, puts you right smack in the middle of mystery. We think about mystery abstractly, but we experience some version of it regularly. Rather than fearing it, we can trust that writing gives us a lot of room to explore and find our way. Believing that our fifth brain can use the lostness as fuel for our texts, we can turn the mystery into something shareable.

Almost thirty years after that night on the buses, I can vouch that I've been lost a lot. In 2018, I found myself petting a neighbor's cat in a borrowed flat on an island in the Mediterranean. I was on sabbatical, writing this book about writing, which is something I'd never done before. I had learned some of the dirt roads I could see in the valley below, and I had eaten at some of the places in the town across the way, but I was alone. Every decision about every second of the day was mine. I knew no one in that town. The hours to eat were different, and the clock was global. I drove on the other side of the street than I'm used to, and there wasn't internet in the house where I stayed. Since I was overseas, with a ten–hour time difference, all the people I might have called for comfort were asleep. On top of this unknowing, when I was writing, I was at a new crossroads every hour, pondering which way to turn. I was both vulnerable and powerful. When people want to hear about this trip, more than anything, I want to show them my pulse and say, *I felt very alive.* This is what writing feels like, a lot of the time. Being present and alive despite not knowing, despite fear, despite invisibility.

Not-knowing is an uncomfortable crossroads. Recently, a friend texted, "I can't write a novel! I have no idea what I'm doing." She sounded exactly like everyone I ever knew who was writing a novel. Or frankly, any kind of book. But if you knew how to write your text already, there would be no need to go to the crossroads in the first place; you wouldn't be traveling.

You must make your writing a beloved, an act that you want to visit, that is worth the getting lost. If you think your writing is an adversary withholding something from you, you annihilate the pleasure of discovering, the intimate joy of the work. Would you rather risk making a text that takes you somewhere you didn't know you wanted to go, or would you prefer to give up and slide back into a comfortable town of streets that you know and keep doing the things you know how to do? It's a choice that you can make, and either choice is doable.

Being in relationship and witnessing the lostness of others can drive us into new material, too. When I was in my thirties, my boyfriend was diagnosed with a brain tumor. He'd been having headaches. It turned out to be a golf-ball-sized tumor in the personality sector of his brain, grade four glioblastoma, in the frontal lobe. We became obscured by his tumor. He and I lived together, made calls to doctors, waited for appointments, and paused our lives. Except that we didn't pause because you can't. I won a literary prize the same day that the neurologist called my boyfriend to confirm the presence of the tumor. Someone paid me $7,000 for a single story and an hour later, there was my boyfriend's voice on the phone, stunned, telling me he was going to have brain surgery.

I wasn't the one who had a brain tumor, but it took over my life, too. The night of his surgery, I slept on a chair in a hospital waiting room where other strangers slept. It was a lightless, windowless room, ripe with the haunts of terrible news. I waited, lost in the dark under a puffy black coat, unable to sleep. Finally,

I got up and went to a hallway with light and started to write. In fact, out of that experience I wrote two pieces, a nonfiction essay, and a short story. Writing is available at the crossroads, even if all you have to talk about is being lost, and what crossroads you're currently facing.

Now that I've trained myself to pay attention to lostness, I can see that I've always studied this inexplicable element of human life. When I was a teenager, a friend of mine spent a couple of nights in a jail for a drugstore holdup. Afterwards, she told me of her jail experience, "I was hungry, and finally they brought me some lunch, but my soup had a live worm in it." She kept mentioning the worm. She was more disappointed about that worm than she was about having a police record, or about the fact that she was making disastrous life choices. She died tragically, not long after. I think of that invertebrate as a symbol of something gone very wrong in her life, the symbol of her lostness. That soup worm has been curling and uncurling in my imagination for over forty years, waiting for its story. (And maybe this is it.)

Your own heart can be lost. Sometimes you are overwhelmed by emotions, relationships, experiences. If you choose to write through your grief or anger or yearning or embarrassment or lostness, writing can find you and promote real evolution. There can be immense freedom in giving the lostness of emotions over to a text.

Once, I had the most confusing fight with a partner. It was a mysterious and frustrating argument. I couldn't even figure out what we were fighting about, but my partner's anger was vivid. We were on vacation in Mexico with my parents, so the argument took place in whispered bursts or quick walks.

The last afternoon we were there, I sat out on the porch, roiling with anger, steaming from the inside, and then I remembered a character that I'd been working on who was as anguished and furious as I was. I hadn't written this character's despair yet because I didn't know how to get in. But that afternoon, on the porch of that rented place in Mexico, I wrote an excruciating scene. I put every scrap of fury and despair into my character, Antwerp. Antwerp and I understood each other that day. I let him betray his best friend, and I understood why he did it. When I read that scene now, I think, *Oh, Antwerp.* Also, I think, *That's right, Antwerp, go all the way out on that limb of despair.* I found my balance in that writing. I gave my confusion to Antwerp and let him show me how troubled things were in my life, too.

The feeling of being lost, in its many variations, is often excruciating. There is an acute and unbearable quality to the human condition sometimes. But we can trust ourselves to find a way. We have our own smart, sensible, creative fifth brains. The human brain works on a subconscious, reflexive basis. The brain does this all the time with the body. The brain doesn't ask you to think consciously about breathing or about beating your heart. The biological brain does all the work and leaves your subconscious free to imagine, to dream up worlds, people, music, paintings into being. Some part of us is always listening. The fifth brain/imagination/dreaming brain needs thinking time and space in which to flourish, and sometimes even the need for patience leaves you feeling lost.

This entire planet of humans was lost during the Coronavirus pandemic. Information poured through our devices and our conversations were obsessed with the right way to handle the virus. As of this writing 6,833,388 people died from Covid worldwide and new (lesser) variants still emerge. How many family members, coworkers and friends are still in the space of lostness that is mourning? How did we, do we, return to our lives? How much are we changed? How are our values changed? People are changing jobs, moving, ending relationships, falling in love, mourning, suffering long-Covid symptoms. If ever there was an emphatic example of the ways that lostness invades a life, this is it. Many writers and artists talk about not being able to make work during this period. Sometimes, when you are lost, you have to stop and wait until you are found. Stop and wait until you have enough heart to write things down. And then the world opens, and we breathe each other's air again and some of us begin to write.

This existence is a series of crossroads. There are many ways to lose yourself. It is the writer's secret that we can find ourselves, our ferocity, our stories, our questions, our answers, if we accept that being lost is also being alive. If we take our lostness to the page and see where to go from there.

Do you feel like writing?

Play with the idea of a crossroad (roads that intersect and force you to choose a path). You might be looking at physical, psychic, emotional lostness, or otherwise. It might be a literal crossroad, where you write the choices on a wooden sign that looms over you/the character. Are you surrounded by corn fields? A city? Are you on Mars? Do you know what you will do next?

Do you feel like writing?
Write about a decision your narrator is facing without any
mention of a crossroad.

Do you feel like writing?
Write about the inevitability of lostness.

Do you feel like writing?
Where in the body do you store your lostness? Write about it.

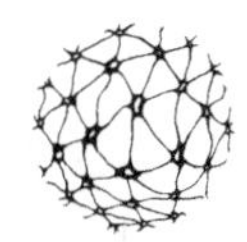

CHAPTER SEVEN

Dream of the Giant Blue Eye

Science tells us that everyone dreams, from the time they are born until the time they die. Some people believe that they don't dream, but science notes that most people do even if they don't remember their dreams. It's estimated that in an average lifespan, people dream anywhere from six to twenty-five years of their lives. Whether you will dream for six years, ten years, or twenty years, there is a lot there to harness for writing: images, startling events, new characters, concepts.

During a period when I was trying to give up writing because I blamed it for not saving me from the difficulties of life, I dreamt I was napping. I woke in the dream to find a version of myself, three stories tall, staring at me through my bedroom window. The Big Me was impatient. She insisted that I leave whatever I was doing and join her. She peered in the window with a massive blue eye. She blinked. She was wearing hiking clothes and it was raining lightly. In the dream, I rolled away from the window and closed my eyes to go back to sleep. When I awoke again, she was glaring in at me with her clear blue eye, outraged now, squinting.

"Come," she demanded. I shook my head, slightly, no.

She shrugged, her lips flat with disgust. She turned and moved away, as if to leave me behind.

I saw her body, all three stories of it, my head and my torso and my giant story-high legs, headed for the pine tree forest behind my ugly apartment building in North Carolina. She was my writing self, and she was going to leave me. The biggest part of me was leaving.

"Wait! Please! Wait! I'm coming!" I called, and I sprang from my bed and ran down the stairs into the rain after her.

Actually, I tried to give up writing twice, both times in my twenties. I suspected that I wouldn't make much money at it, that people wouldn't understand my choice, that it would be hard, personal work, that I'd have to struggle and scrape to make time for it, that I would have to make choices on behalf of a largely intangible art. The three-story-writer-me doesn't care about any of this. Did I write after that dream? I did. I was scared back into it, and in fact, in the writing, I found my way through the problems I was having and moved into a sweeter period. I call this the Dream of the Giant Blue Eye. It is one of my origin stories. Did it matter to my life that I wrote? It did. Writing saves me, every time.

For years I've been thinking about Joseph Campbell's discussions with interviewer, Bill Moyers, where Campbell said, "This is the time you get into when you go to sleep and have a dream that talks about permanent conditions within your own psyche as they relate to the temporal conditions of your life right now."

Out of all the approaches to dreaming, this seems to me a believable way to think about dreams. What would you say are your permanent conditions of the psyche, aspects that are steady and permanent in your personality, whether positive or negative? What temporal conditions of your life are you experiencing currently? Campbell is talking about dreaming as a lens to peer at our overall vs. current personhood. Who is the dream talking to about these conditions? I propose that dreaming is the fifth brain talking to its owner.

Dreams are mysterious, even in neuroscience to this day. In 5th century BC, Plato thought dreams were physiologically produced, while Herodotus thought they reflected daily thoughts. In the 21st century, dream researchers continue to pin down the biological structures of dream, although there is no one explanation of their purpose. Usually, one of eight possible explanations for dreams arises in dream neuroscience articles. In educator Amy Adkins' TED talk, "Why Do We Dream?" she presents this set of accepted theories about dreams. In short, dreams either cause the dreamer to fulfill wishes, remember things, forget things, work, rehearse, heal things or problem solve. No one agrees which of these theories is the "final word" on dreams because no one can agree on any final word. This only makes dreams seem more special, an incredible mystery embedded in an act that humans and animals do all the time. Nobody knows! We've been guessing at the same question at least since the 5th century BC.

Carl Jung believed that the material of the dream is striving to be known to the conscious dreamer. He writes, "Dream symbols are the essential message carriers from the instinctive to the rational parts of the human mind, and their interpretation enriches the poverty of consciousness so that it learns to understand again the forgotten language of instincts." Are we stopping the message carrier at the door when we dismiss our dreams? Often, we say, *No thanks, instinctive brain, I have all the images I need right now over here in my rational brain. I'm balancing my budget and counting calories and I have my chores and schedule and nothing else is needed for life.* I see Jung's "poverty of consciousness" as a life that doesn't honor imagination. Dreams and daydreams, creativity, and visions, are part of living essence. To me, this is the "quality of life." I believe that accessing dreams (and by proxy accessing the fifth brain) connects a person to "the forgotten language of instincts."

Some writers dismiss the idea of including dreams in their writing, but dreams are a part of the human condition. Dreams appear in my characters' lives, but only when I suspect that a dream might have really come to them. Dreams, since they lack chronology and rationality, can be hard to read in large chunks in a text, but parts of daydreams or REM dreams, flickeringly, can be used as symbol in a story: an army, a stray cat, a giant self.

For centuries, authors have used dreams to highlight the larger theme of a text to motivate or illustrate a character. In Homer's *Odyssey*, Penelope has three significant dreams, one of which offers foreshadowing for impending action. Penelope dreams of an eagle killing twenty geese, which is widely interpreted to mean that Odysseus (the eagle) will return to kill her suitors (the geese), which indeed he does.

In the early pages of *Anna Karenina,* Leo Tolstoy shows us Anna seeing a peasant carrying a sack. Throughout the book, Anna Karenina dreams of a peasant carrying a sack without ever remembering that she'd seen it. Here, Tolstoy illustrates a conscious daytime image moving into dream (unremembered by the dreamer). Then he has Anna Karenina interpret her dream for the reader as a dark omen. She fulfills this omen with her suicide. The dream moves the plot inexorably forward.

My favorite dream in literature, in Fyodor Dostoyevsky's *Brothers Karamazov*, serves to move the plot of the book forward by illuminating various levels of a character's personality. At this point in the book, it is implicated that the character, Mitya Karamazov, is the murderer of his father. Mitya has a dream that implies a turn in his life. In the dream, he is in a carriage driving past a burned-out village where women and children are standing, blue and shivering. Mitya asks the driver what has happened. When the driver points out the obvious, that they have been burned out and are freezing and starving, Mitya swears that he will work against such bad fortune "with all the recklessness of the Karamazovs." Dostoyevsky reveals the complexity of Mitya's internal world through this dream. It is a subconscious event that invokes sympathy. Mitya's avowal to help others implies a burgeoning morality in his character and the reference to his family's nature implies loyalty to his family. This bit of dream becomes, for the reader, a vote for Mitya's good heartedness. A dream that works towards his defense.

Another book, *Madeline Is Sleeping*, by Sarah Shun-Lien Bynum, offers a narrative that flickers between the "real" life and the "dream" life in such an entangled way that it makes the reader feel as though they, like the protagonist, Madeline, are dreaming. The whole time I read this book, I imagined all the events occurring in a sepia tone. Like a dream, the book travels in fragments so that even after reading the book multiple times, I can recite images or characters more than I could relate any defined plot and yet, this book is a place I've wanted to revisit many times.

My own characters dream the way that I do, in ways that affect their waking lives. I wrote a novella titled after a dream, *Doctor Porchiat's Dream*, and in it, a doctor in the superstitious 1720s performs his first autopsy, an emotionally disturbing and scientifically thrilling act. Doctor Porchiat has a dream after the autopsy, and he confides it to an unknown interviewer, "In the dream I found it, tucked away behind the heart. The soul. I knew I'd never seen anything like it. I snipped it free from the small web of arteries, washed it clean of blood, and set it in an enamel bowl. It was tiny, parchment colored, yellow-clear, and gilled, little shutters on either side." In this dream, I present the soul as a literal human organ. This is not a story of magical realism, so I didn't want to make a soul-organ real, but I wanted the suggestion in the story. I wanted it to exist in the reader's mind, so I gave it to Porchiat's subconscious. This dream marks the beginning of the doctor's inquiry into autopsy, but also is harbinger of that which will end his career. The dream moves the plot forward.

There are ways of intentionally dreaming into your writing, too. A long time ago, I had one of those financial bottoming outs that can mark an artist's life. I was living in my friend's basement, cleaning attics, working as a handy woman, driving all over the state as a teaching artist. I was falling in love with someone at this time, too. I was, in every way, tumultuous, chaotic, unsettled. But I knew that I had to write. The need was urgent. There was never enough time. I would sit down with my precious hours and start to work. Within an hour, I would fall asleep. Right there, sitting upright at the desk, I would fall asleep. Inwardly screaming at the injustice of such biology, I fought it. I tried to think, to write, to see beyond seeing which is what writing takes for me. I fell asleep anyways. My pen was always still in my hand, my head on the pages I'd written before, and I would sleep, though not for very long. Ten minutes or so. I'd wake up furious and self-castigating. After this happened twice, though, I noticed that when I awoke, I awoke with an idea, and often, the hand was lifting the pen and beginning to write, and the idea was there. I'd dreamt it. It was as though my brain needed to shut down the parts that were overheated, over-anxious, overworking, overthinking. My brain shut those down and woke something else, something deeper. This method of allowing sleep has become a ritual that I still don't like, but I do observe. When I am writing now and feel the sleep coming on, I meekly set my head down on the desk and make sure my pen is ready.

The surrealist artist, Salvador Dali, wrote about a technique, "slumber with a key" as one of his fifty secrets of "magic craftsmanship." Dali claims that the greatest potential inspiration lay in the dream. "What you prevent yourself from doing and force yourself not to do, the dream will do with all the lucidity of desire," he advises. Dali instructs novices to sit in a comfortable armchair, "preferably Spanish" and advises them to hold a key with thumb and forefinger above an overturned plate. When they fall asleep, the clattering will wake them. Then they are to rise and make art. Though my way is less dramatic and less Spanish, it is the same fifth brain sort of principle, trusting that the art will come.

Other writers describe fifth brain revelations in ways that seem positively dreamlike. In her book, *Still Writing*, Dani Shapiro describes the moment of losing yourself in writing as having "a quality of déjà vu," meaning that it comes from a place so burrowed in the brain and cells that it seems you already knew it.

Dreams are a place from which much intelligence comes. The Khomani San Bushmen say, "There is a dream dreaming us." Dreaming is a facet of the human imagination. We couldn't ever make any sense of this statement without engaging our imagination. What is a *dream*? Who is *us*? Who, other than you, is in charge of your dreaming? Who, other than you, is in charge of your writing? What if we replaced the word "dream" in that sentence with its source: there is an *imagination imagining* us. Isn't dwelling in the imagination a kind of dreaming? Isn't it our own imagination pouring endless new variations of images and sounds across our mind's eye as we sleep?

In 2013, artist and novelist, Audrey Niffenger, had a retrospective of her artwork, *Awake in the Dream World* at the National Museum of Women in the Arts, and in an article where she discusses the origins of her art-making, she states, "I am still on the same path I first took when I was a child, awake in the dream world, making and unmaking that world with black lines on pieces of paper, never knowing, always wondering." A life spent exploring imagination is a life of being awake in the dream world.

When I was writing the first pages of this book, I had a dream where a 25-foot-long bright red Gila monster demanded that I build wings for it. In the dream, I sketched out the design for the wings and put together a team to make them. There was organization and work and everyone in the dream was engaged and happy. When I woke, I found that a thousand tangled concerns had been cleared from my brain, making me ready for writing. My fifth brain makes valuable images big so that I can't ignore them. I write these things down, I listen, I let my fifth brain work on the meanings.

I'm a daydreamer, too. I like to sit and look out the window. This is where a lot of stories start for me. Sometimes when I'm out in the world, too. Recently, I was in a high Colorado mountain town, looking across a field of snow flickered with tree shadows, and I could hear a murmured conversation. This conversation has since turned into a short story where a fairy godmother and a witch discuss their greatest failures. I have trained myself to understand that if I free my brain from anxious looping about everyday matters, I can be rewarded with visions from my own imagination, which is always up there, always in there, always with me.

I think we should revere our dreams and daydreams and I think we should do this for each other. What if, instead of impatience when someone wants to tell a dream, we listened and asked questions, and helped each other find the messages embedded there?

I wish I could go back in time and tell my second-grade teacher that I was not just daydreaming and that I would not "lose my head if it weren't screwed on" but that I was, in fact, communing with my fifth brain. An act that has become the heart of my entire career.

Do you feel like writing?

If you remember your dreams and write them down, take one image from a dream and let it speak. Maybe it's a teapot or a crow or a snake. Give it a voice and let it tell you its story.

Do you feel like writing?

Write about the "permanent conditions within your own psyche." (Define this however you want.) Now write about the "temporal conditions of your life right now." (Define this however you want.) Or do this for a character.

Writing's First Home
Is Inside the Physical Body

We are animals. The human species. We have needs for food and water and shelter. Beyond those basics, our brains have their specific neural patterns, about 85 billion neurons firing, that we have developed based on our senses, imagination, feelings, learnings, and memories. These particularities are what we can trust make our art individual to us. But to facilitate this art, we need to be aware of our specific needs, noting the places and rituals we require to help us work. Some of us will have lots of needs, some of us have minimalist needs. This is not a place for judgment or improvement, but a place to learn our patterns. Human patterns are not absolutes, and if we are always changing (and we are), then we should expect this work of studying our own patterns to be a lifelong endeavor.

Evaluating our patterns is intellectual, analytical work. It is part of your art form, knowing what kind of atmosphere can help you write, what tools you need, what sets the foundation for you to sink into your own imagination and language. This chapter invites you to examine what comes naturally, to observe your animal-writer-self. Often when we talk about our writing habits, we first note what we "should do" or describe what other people do and shame-facedly describe how we don't do that. As my friend, K, always says to me, what if we reframe this? What if we look at this from a different perspective? This reframing technique is incredibly freeing. What if instead of us failing to live up to other's writing habits, we celebrate our own? Maybe you procrastinate because that works for you. Maybe you lose your notes because you needed to. Maybe you write an outline because that works for you. Maybe you never write an outline because that doesn't work for you. Maybe you stay up until four am because that is the time you are most creative. Rock it out! Do your thing! Pay attention and know what your thing is and do it!

Examine your patterns for inspiration. Do you know what enlivens your imagination? Reading works for me, prose and poetry. Jazz helps a lot, too, and other music with rising and falling action (few or no words, or I'll unconsciously take dictation). Looking at photographs or artwork inspires me. Talking to other writers. Hiking or being alone outside. A thought-provoking movie. Camping. Being in a library or bookstore. Taking notes on books about writing or philosophy or art making. If you don't have any rituals in this way, think about when you feel engaged or excited and incorporate those activities into your writing time. I know if I'm going to see an art film or a foreign film that I'll need to bring a notebook for scribbling ideas in the dark. Similarly, when I'm hiking, I always stop along the way to jot notes down. Not about the movie or the trail, but regarding what these things provoke in my own imagination. I've studied my patterns, so I know how to get myself into a writing mode when I need.

There might be repetitive motivations. Once I walked past a music store where music was piped into the street. They were playing a song that sounded like the island I was writing about in a novel. The violinist, Anne Akiko Myers, was playing "Birds in Warped Time II," and as I listened, I saw a figure running through light and shadow in a pinewoods swamp. I walked into the store and bought the album. I listened to that album for years while I wrote and revised that book. The first few notes of that album can snap me right out my ordinary life and hurl me into that fictional world. I can see the shadow and light every time that song begins.

Where and when do you like to write? Over the years I have taught myself to write anytime and anywhere with any utensil at hand, but I have my preferences and ways that writing comes easier for me. I like to write in the morning before my brain latches on to the ordinary chores of the day. I write by hand, first. I like smooth paper and fine ball point pens when possible. I like to take notes and listen to music and have little white lights on in my study. You have to know your patterns of contentment to recreate them. Study what lights up your own fifth brain and develop rituals around those elements so that your animal self can sink into the work. Having said that, we must resist rigidity, too. When these things are happening, I'm most at ease but if I waited for only these patterns to be in place, I'd never get my writing done. Making a path for your writing is critical and being willing to be interrupted by your writing is valuable, too.

Author Monique Truong, in an interview with *Diacritics*, writes of her method of transition: "Ritual (a long walk beforehand, a cup of roasted rice tea during, a salutary nod to my literary heroes, Gertrude Stein and Marguerite Yourcenar, whose works in various forms occupy a place of honor on my writing desk right now) is about the physical, intellectual and emotional transition that needs to take place before I can shed my day-to-day self and become my writing self." Truong also talks about having to wear shoes while writing because what is happening is so out of control that she feels she needs to be ready for emergency. Her discussion of the physical, intellectual, and emotional transition that we make between our ordinary selves and our writing selves depicts an intensity. It can be a difficult transition, so we need to lay the foundation for our own success.

There's lots of advice out there and this is why it's so valuable to figure out what works for you. Recently, someone asked if I thought it was lame to follow Julia Cameron's *The Artist's Way* advice, writing three pages a day (not lame!). I was talking to someone else on another day, who was feeling guilty because she didn't write three pages a day, as recommended in that same book (not lame either!). There is no prescription for your writing life but the one you create. No pattern is inherently lame. No pattern is required from the outside world. No one technique will work for everyone. Try things. Be gentle.

Each text, too, has its own needs and systems. Sometimes stories come to me in a matter of days. Conversely, I've worked on books for years. I make it complicated sometimes, but a text simply wants to grow itself sentence by sentence, to become a complete, whole creature. It won't be forced, and it won't always develop the same way previous texts have. It's useful to understand each text's process, to understand where you are in a draft, and to know how this process changes from text to text.

Once I was having trouble finishing a novella-length fairy tale I'd been working on, and I told a friend that I thought maybe it was two books. They pointed out that I was probably just eager to have something to show for the work I'd done all summer. It surprised me that someone else could have a correct insight about my work, that I could be wrong. But it wasn't that I didn't know the truth of my impatience, it was more like I was refusing to listen to something I didn't want to hear. This conversation helped me learn that I am impatient when the circle of writing and reading is only half-built. I get lonely in these worlds of my invention. I want people on my islands, in my desert, in my church-turned-hospital, in my fairy tale underworld. I want to see how my inventions look through their eyes, but I must be patient and let the text take the time it needs to be born.

Another thing I've learned about my patterns is that I need to show up to the page regularly, or I get cranky. Sometimes I am just there to noodle around with setting, or tweak earlier pages, or fix those weird spaces that I've created because I can't adjust to single spaces between sentences. Maybe I'm there to interview a character. Maybe I'm there to check for and delete any uses of the word "suddenly." Maybe I drag my notebook to a restaurant and realize that I'm there to order lunch and wait for the next idea to appear. It's excruciating. I don't want to diminish how painful and laborious this is. But also, it's how the shape of the work finds its true nature without the ego of the writer mucking up the process. One of the patterns I need to be aware of is "no-pattern." I must remember that my particular process is widely varied.

It is hard to be in control, moving forward, while at the same time being gentle and letting go. A writer needs to allow for gentleness and encouragement to call upon all the days, weeks, months, years it might take something to emerge into its full, authentic shape. This is the hardest thing about writing some-times, even though the whole point is watching the unfolding, inventing the unfolding, birthing the unfolding, beholding, rejoicing. Even though the point is the writing.

Can you recognize when your brain is ready to deliver a text to you? Do you have rituals around the writing that you can turn to when you have an idea? When a short story comes to me, I know what it feels like. The sign is never the same, but the feeling is the same. An excitement. A curiosity, a hum, a vibration. It might start with a title, or a setting, or a name, or a character, or a situation. If I can, I stop everything and tend to it. If I can't, I make notes and hold a pocket of space in my brain for it until I can write it down. If it's a short piece, I might be able to pound out a draft in a matter of days if I tend to it. I know when I've figured out the ending to a story, because there is a feeling of walls crumbling towards me, a satisfying, giving-way sensation. It reveals, pours forth, and I must catch it with my pen. These are my fifth brain's signs and I know them because I've studied them.

As paramount as it is to know what excites your imagina-tion, it's good to observe what deadens your imagination. What obstructs it? Sometimes, I'm not really in a headspace to write. I'm anxious or distracted or overwhelmed by other aspects of my life. I could slog through, force it, but there is no point if I am not fully present. These events are not inherently good or bad, but I know they are not conducive for my writing. Knowing this saves me a lot of grief.

Another aspect to analyze are your patterns as a reader. What do you read? How do you find out about new stuff to read? Where do you read? Do you read hardcovers or paperbacks or e-books or articles in print or articles online or graphic novels? What are your favorite moments in reading? Can you name ways that reading has changed you as a writer, or how it might inform your work? What makes you set down someone else's book and write?

A good book can really set me off into writing. Once I was reading two books about massive political regimes being upset by revolution. One is from the point of view of the revolutionary who has lost his taste for the violence he must perpetrate (*Courilof Affair* by Irene Nemirovsky), and one is from the point of view of a nobleman in Moscow, who has accepted the judgment passed onto him by the Bolsheviks (*Gentlemen in Moscow* by Amor Towles). Suddenly, reading these two books at once helped me with a soldier character that I'd been stuck on for a while. My original intention for my story was to examine how people, communities, and individuals heal after global wars and plagues. But the answer that this character revealed is that sometimes they don't heal. My character is irrevocably altered by his experiences in World War I. This isn't what I wanted to write (here's another of my patterns I need to be aware of, ignoring what the text wants). I wanted to save him. But these other books showed me his true condition. Just as the revolutionary has been trapped in his life of violence, just as Count Rostov is stuck in the Metropole, my character, too, is trapped in the larger machinations of his world and time period.

In fact, I've always been fascinated by war novels. War is one of my subjects, probably because it's such a crux of human despair and hope. I discovered that this is one of my own writing subjects by observing my patterns of reading and refraining from judgment. There's information stored in your reading preferences about you as a thinker, about you as a writer. I know that what I read is driven by my fifth brain, so I pay attention to which books draw my attention.

Sometimes the necessary ritual is waiting. My friend, C, wrote that she's set aside a novel that needs more time. She wrote, "Anyway, it feels a little weird/empty. Not bad, just kind of taking a breath. It's like the exhale. I'm waiting to fill up again." It sounds so hard, waiting to fill up. What do we do in such moments? What patterns can we fall back on? How do we even know what we're waiting for? The waiting might become the ritual of doing-something-else. If you know what patterns feed your writing, go to those activities instead of trying to force the lines. When I read my work and can't find a single redemptive quality in any sentence, I know it is time to step away. I force myself to leave the room, pick up a book, watch a movie, or clean the house. I find something pleasurable or useful to do, which will relieve the sting of having to be patient and divert any feeling of failure.

It's not a failure to be a human, and a human is not an art-making robot. There are going to be good days and bad days. Let the animal rest when it needs to and trust that the time will come to write again. Keep the pressure off. Wait to fill up.

Do you feel like writing?
Write a prescription for your writing life for the next week. Prescriptions recommend daily doses, warnings about what kinds of foods you should or should not have, what kinds of activities you should engage in to help the medicine best do its work.

Do you feel like writing?

Daily Steal: Every day for a week, write about something you have seen or heard in the world around you. Observe it in plain detail, give it to a character, or make it a line in a poem.

Do you feel like writing?

Consider your own internal writing rules: First, name the rules you write by. Which ones are helpful and which ones should you shed? Which are the ones you would never break and why? For example, what topics are you not allowed to write about?

CHAPTER NINE

There Is No One Path

In a class workshop once, one student said to another, "This is absolutely your style." I corrected the idea that each of us has only one style. We might. Or we might not. All the styles are free for us to try. Each writer has our own issues and curiosities to explore over a lifetime, and our art will explore these in a variety of ways over time. Instead of claiming one style for life, it might be more appropriate to ask what kind of style does your writing need *right now*? Modernism, post-modernism, post-colonialism, minimalism, maximalism, fabulism. So many -isms! There are ways into different styles. If you like the way something has been written, try modeling it for yourself. How does it feel? How does it serve what you want to write? We are limited in style only by our own belief systems about what we can and cannot try. Be adventurous. Try anything you want!

Whether you study writing formally or not, you can always educate yourself about the vast range of styles available from different time periods, from different cultures through reading widely. Perhaps you need the breadth of "maximalism," where footnotes create meta-commentary in the work of authors like William Gass and Dave Eggers and Ruth Ozeki and Junot Diaz. Perhaps you need to write page-long chapters. Maybe you need to offer visual art mingled with stream of consciousness observations like Claudia Rankine. Perhaps you need to write one-sentence fictions like Lydia Davis. Ocean Vuong blends the lyric with the intimate quality of confiding a story. Maybe you need to include letters, receipts, images. People are out there, owning their art, changing the course of the literary canon. You can be among them. When I started writing, I wanted to write like Raymond Carver. (Carver was considered a minimalist, a label he rejected.) I was devastated when almost all my stories could be categorized as magical realism instead. I gained strength once I leaned into my natural inclinations, and once I understood those, I was free to try other things. Maybe you saw yourself as a poet, but now you need to figure out how to write a novel. Is that allowed? Of course it is. You own your writing life. Make it like you like it.

Who are you as a sentence/line maker these days? In sentence making, I think about visual shape, sound, and meaning, although I have to wait for later drafts to do this kind of work. I think about the form of sentences to emphasize content. I like to mimic the action of the content in the form of the sentence, even if that sentence is going to be buried in a novel of sentences. In fact, I'll spend a whole draft reviewing each sentence shape. I call this draft the "Beautification Draft." I am impatient to get to this draft, but I must wait until I have written the content before I can shape the lines. Then I am impatient to get through this draft because it is weighty work to look at each sentence. Writing isn't easy work, as if we don't know that already.

It is useful and interesting to try out the styles of other authors but do be warned that you can get stuck there if you aren't careful. Remember that you are always looking for your own way through your writing, and trust that your fifth brain will help you. Study the styles of others, put those shapes and forms into your fifth brain and then stop reading those authors' works for a little while. Let your fifth brain parse out what you need for your own work.

We have so many choices. Genre, style, form, sentence shape or line, content, character, point of view, tense, voice, etc. A story can be told any way, and there isn't one right way. In *Steering the Craft*, Ursula Le Guin writes, "Verb tenses have so little connotation of actual present or pastness that they are in most respects interchangeable. . .both present tense and past tense narrative are totally fictive." It makes perfect sense. A fictive tense is always fictive, in fact, so there can be no foregone conclusion about what tense you choose. Thinking about tenses as being interchangeable reminds us that sometimes the limitations we let limit our writing are choices that we are making.

One of the things I'm suggesting, again, regarding choices about language and laws and verbs, is that there aren't absolutes. As I came into my writing life and encountered various authors and instructors and mentors telling me that there is an exact process for how I should write, sometimes I found myself whispering: *bullshit*. The implication that there is an "always" that works for "everyone" is bullshit. Any time you insist that there is an *always,* you exclude someone, you narrow possibility.

We live in an ever-changing world, which requires us to find new ways of expressing new revelations or new movements. In the *London Observer* in 1965, James Baldwin writes about being a black man in a world that doesn't often reflect the language of his life and culture. He says, "My quarrel with the English language has been that the language reflected none of my experience." He found his own patterns, instead, and used them to write with eloquence and force. Did he change the world in doing so? Yes. The risk-taking of writers can move the world forward incrementally.

People wielding "Standard Written English" often reject accents and dialects and vernaculars as symbols of lesser intelligence. As if people speaking in other languages or people speaking accented English as a second or third language are inherently less intelligent! We can recognize that English is a global and fluid language. We have terms for this de-colonizing work around language. Code-meshing recognizes that all language and dialects are inherently complex and valuable. Code-switching observes that there is no such thing as a standard and different dialects and languages can coexist, even in the same text, and still communicate meaning. Language is a living, changing entity, reflecting the identity of humans who use it to communicate.

There are embedded morality and class issues in discussions of language, but all the words belong to you and me. All of them. For example, cussing is part of the language, too. Who decided which words aren't appropriate? Who gets to tell me what language to use? Cuss words belong to us, just like all the other words that haven't been deemed cuss words. People have told me that I shouldn't cuss "when I have the whole English language at my service." In the educational theorist, Sugata

Mitra's, TED talk, "The Hole in the Wall," he relates how the great English empire taught cultures to write and add by hand in the same formulaic way so that we could send our data back to the motherland by ship. In this way, the English embedded their own class system and morals in the hierarchy of language use. How could such an old system still be relevant in the constantly changing communities on this planet? Each of us owns the words! All of them! There are always going to be arguments about that (and issues of class lurk here) but the truth is that no one person or part of society should get to name what kinds of communication are right and wrong. It's fine if people want to use standard written English as I've done in this book (because I'm in my fifties, and I'm white, and it's been ingrained in me). But don't let anyone talk you out of the prize of owning your own communication, not for marketing or image or platform or anything. Be the biggest writer you want to be. Own the whole damn world of language. Change it, even.

And yet! (There's always an "and yet!") There are other complications. There are concerns about using language that stereotypes or appropriates from other cultures and it is your work to be aware of the ramifications of choices you make. If you suspect that you are stereotyping or appropriating in your writing, ask for a sensitivity reading from a friend or peer who will do that for you, or hire one. If you suspect your text is unintentionally privileged or racist or ableist or misogynist or transphobic or homophobic or similarly limited, then it is your responsibility. You can fix it and thus expand your readership. (I am assuming that you would want to, because I'm a humanitarian who believes in human dignity and respect.) It's okay if it happens in your drafts. Drafts allow us the eloquence of growth.

If you don't study craft or other texts, if you aren't reading, then there is no way for you to develop an understanding of the laws you would want to follow, recreate, or break in your own work. We teach our readers how to read our texts within the first few pages. We signal the style the reader can expect and create the laws for our own work. There is not one standard. Writers in India or Syria or the United States might create texts meant to be similar in form (short stories), but due to cultural and geographical and linguistic differences, their stories might be vastly different. Each writer will signal to the reader what to expect.

You might choose to break the norms. You might be someone like Jose Saramago who emulates a version of blindness in his book, *Blindness*, by lack of punctuation and paragraphing, or you might be like Virginia Woolf, depending on the semicolon to create pauses and waves. But if your choices are random or unintentional there will be chaos and incoherence in your text, and if there is, no reader will sustain the reading for long. Opinions are only opinions (including mine). John Gardner writes in *The Art of Fiction* that every use of third person point of view is "sappy." I immediately rebel. Doesn't he dismiss a gazillion wonderful books with this statement? Opinions might be satisfying to express, but do they further creativity? Offer new ideas? Are they there to help you? Think critically about the advice you take, about whether the truth that someone offers you is a limiting idea. There are many belief systems that you can choose from. Philosophies! Pedagogies! Movements! Literary Styles! There is a whole host of wagons for you to climb into or out of, but as a broad-minded writer, at least try to refrain from the mistake of assuming that your wagon is the only one that matters.

Organic beings are not binary. It takes practice to resist absolutes. It takes courage to resist them. It takes curiosity to step beyond them. Is third person point of view always sappy? Try it out. If you find yourself naturally gravitating towards first person, present tense, follow the impulse. Second person, past tense? No punctuation? Read books that shook the status quo with their language. Read Zora Neale Hurston. Read James Joyce. Read Gloria Anzaldua, Bernadette Mayer, Leonora Carrington, Angela Carter, and thousands of others. Try things. You can always revise, alter, change the language. You can be one of the ones who changes the status quo. It is up to you, as a writer, to make the language reflect your experience.

Do you feel like writing?
Find an example of a piece of your writing and study your style:
- *Word choice patterns.* Do you use long words or short words? Curse words? Multiple languages?
- *Grammatical patterns.* Semi colons? Soft commas for a pause?
- *Sentence structure patterns.* Do you use long sentences or short? Do you like clauses?
- *Paragraph structure patterns.* Do you use long paragraphs or short? Do you break dialogue with gesture?
- *Narrative structure patterns.* What is the mix of action, dialogue, interior monologue, interior emotion, description, and narrative summary in your writing?

Do you feel like writing?
Make a list of absolutes that you believe in.

Do you feel like writing?

Try naming your own patterns for drafts. For example, here are the ones I used for one book-length project:

1. Handwritten Draft with first sets of ideas and scenes
2. First Typed and Printed Draft
3. Tense Check Draft
4. Structural Check Draft: looking for missing scenes
5. Handwrite Missing Scenes Draft
6. Type New Scenes and Print Draft
7. Read Aloud Draft
8. Structural Check Draft: pacing and structure only
9. Whites of the Eyes Draft: Are the characters alive?
10. Beautification Draft: language review, sentence structures
11. Reader Response Draft
12. Development with Reader Input Draft
13. Polishing Draft
14. Repeat any of the above as needed as many times as needed.

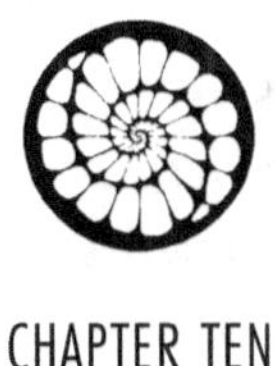

CHAPTER TEN

Every Artist
Exists in Community

The main thing is that you must always, always, talk to writers. Beginners and famous writers and emerging authors alike. They're your people. Read their work. Think about what they are doing. Tell them what you like about what they are doing. Be gracious. Don't be suspicious, jealous, resentful. You want them to do well, to be well, because they are your people. There is always something to talk about between writers. You might find the answer to a problem you've been chewing on, the encouragement you've craved, a new book to read (usually a list of many books). It doesn't matter what they write, you will have something in common with them. Don't be snobbish. Don't be superior. Resist power dynamics and momentary irritations. Take suggestions with a grain of salt. Allow yourself the pleasure of the writing people when you can, because so much of the time, you'll be alone, sometimes confused, doubtful that you are doing anything right in your writing.

We need to actively build a community of readers, especially if we aren't involved in any kind of academic or community-based writing programs. I have found that over the years I've needed a broad variety of community. When I was young, I needed people to show me how to live an artist's life without simply modeling the proletarian work ethic (which doesn't work for my art's demands). I needed experienced writing mentors. Now that I'm older, I need people who keep art at the center of their lives, and people who love to read. I read published work as well as new manuscripts by burgeoning writers. I am mentored by reading work at every stage of its making.

Another surprise that I discovered is that you might find mentors anywhere. The first community college class that I ever taught was for a group of women, ages 16-70. One of these women and I responded similarly to everything. We gasped at the same things, laughed at the same things, were surprised by the same things. I knew this was meaningful. After the class was over, I contacted her and asked if she wanted to write together. She said yes. K and her husband, S, were musicians fully ensconced in the art life. I was K's mentor in writing, and then I ended up doing odd jobs for them for years, and they became mentors for my art life.

That first summer I came to work in their garden. I remember working with K in the flower beds, weeding, adding rich black soil. Tall scarlet and bronze irises towered over us. Bees and monarch butterflies fluttered past. K's small grey terrier barked at bugs. Over our heads, S's trumpet spooled jazz from a wooden-framed window. The music wound over our heads and through the garden into the hundred-foot pines beyond. This,

I thought, is the artist's life. These artists practiced every day, made art every day. They took time for lunch and conversation. They didn't care how a day was spent, in what order things got done. Sometimes all artwork stopped because some other project needed doing. K taught piano. S worked on financial stuff. They wrote songs, practiced. They sat down for elaborate lunches on the back porch in the middle of the day and told stories. They laughed. They fought. They listened to music. They got inspired. They got depressed. They made art. Those stories, those lunches, taught me how to prioritize art, how to carry it in my cells, how to trust my instincts. They mentored me into myself, into the person writing this book.

People naturally turn to classes, schools, degrees for mentors, but that relationship is intentionally confined to a period of time rather than the decades or half centuries you might be writing. It's helpful to remember that mentors come in all shapes and forms, and you will need them all. They will look different and have large and small roles that keep you centered in your writing self. Take some of mine, for example. Recently and without warning, a high school friend sent me a story I'd published in our high school magazine. It was hugely inspirational to remember myself this way, as a person who has always written. That high school friend, sending it, was a mentor, reminding me where I've been. My college buddy's wife, B, was one of the first readers of this book draft and when she read it, she sent me a hundred dollars just so that I would know that she believed in it. That's mentoring, too. Regularly, I share manuscripts and readings with my grad school pals. At this point, we've been watching each other's writing change and grow for twenty-five years. They mentor me all the time. When I lived in Tucson, I was part of a literary nonprofit. I became close friends with the people who ran this center, and I joined the board. As we studied how to support other artists and keep our own writing lives bright, these people became part of my permanent writing family. We mentored each other and still do, even though we live in different places now. My sister is a digital artist and watching her art grow and change from the time we were children is a constant kind of mentoring and encouragement. Now I understand that I will always be gathering my writing community, as long as I live. When people understand what you love most in the world, and when they share this love, it is easier to build connection, to share lives, and create these othered families for your art life.

You need to learn your own writing heart, your own intentions, too. You should consider all the advice offered to you, because there will be plenty, but learn to keep your own counsel. Writers need to learn to discern between advice that resonates and advice that doesn't. You can reject what doesn't feel right, even if later, you realize that it was right. There's no winning or losing, if someone gives you advice that you hate and then you end up taking it. There's no loss of face in taking someone else's advice. The most essential relationship in your writing is always between you and your work, what will most help you write the work that you mean to write.

People don't always understand your choices and decisions about your texts, and this is fine. A friend once asked me about my choice of third person point of view in a novel. With the espresso machine buzzing behind her, my papers sitting dully white and angular on the table in front of me, I couldn't remember, and I felt panicked. A day or so later, I remembered the reasons for my choice. I wanted to call up this friend and explain, but I realized that I didn't have to, because I'm the one who needs to know.

No one else. We must be careful not to give the power away. If I can explain my choices to myself, that is enough.

Your own characters or texts can mentor you, too. I invite characters to the page to converse with me. More than once, I've written myself into a scene with my character, Doctor Porchiat, where he and I sit down to coffee (or whiskey), and I ask him advice about writing or my life. He never fails to give me amazing advice. He knows what I need to hear. I know, intellectually, that he's me, but I feel like his voice accesses fifth brain wisdom that I can't always tap in my ordinary, non-writing self. In another version of this technique, I'll put a character on a stage where they can stand under the spotlight and tell me all sorts of things that I didn't know about themselves. Writing these scenes allows the character to speak from the place where you know them best and where they are at their best, from the page.

After many good and less wonderful writing groups, I've found a small group, just three people, E and S and myself. We are an unlikely combination of ages and experiences, and we all have different reading backgrounds. We're firstly prose writers, fiction and essays, but sometimes we bring poems to our meetings. It's nothing short of magic that it works, and it works so well that we agreed to keep it to ourselves. When you find a good support system like this it's extremely valuable and should be protected.

Here's an example of how this group works at its best. In one meeting, E told me that I should consider getting rid of the aliens in a short story I'd been working on for a year. He said this was one of the hardest stories he'd had to advise me on. Our other group member, S, disagreed. She said, "I think this story is close to being finished." E explained why he thought the aliens shouldn't be there. I could see the versions of the story he suggested. I told E that I really appreciated his ideas and his honesty. I was not ready to get rid of the aliens, even if I should. I might get rid of them in a couple of years, and then he would be right. But they were still my favorite part of that story, and I would probably have to kill the whole story if I took his suggestion, and I didn't want to kill the story. Besides, it has at least one reader. S likes it. Well, two readers, because I like it, too. After this, E smiled and nodded, and we moved onto his work next. There was no bitterness, no recrimination. There was no need for emotion around his suggestion because I trust him, and I know that he wants the best for my work and for me, as a writer. He trusts me, too, and knows that I want the best for his work and for his life as a writer, so we went forward. My readers do not give me different advice because they want to please me or upset me. It is purely based on what they've read, what they like, who they are as readers and writers. It is my job to take all of this into account and make the decisions I need to about the work. I always have the prerogative to keep or discard their advice.

It's a challenge to learn the difference between simple defensiveness and a need to think more about advice. How stubborn you are about advice is up to you. Where you'll bend. You'd be surprised. Once I got rid of three chapters that I'd kept for ten years. I was surprised when I finally decided to axe them. It was a good decision. That phrase, "kill your sweethearts," used to confuse me because what if everything is a sweetheart? But what it really means is: be flexible. Sometimes you can't bend. Sometimes you need to wait. Sometimes you need to wait ten years. Often, you need to be led into a different kind of thinking, and this takes mentors or readers or time or your own willingness to reevaluate.

We must remember that our readers are not us. They do not think the same thoughts, have the exact same feelings, know our history of associations. Author Raymond Obstfeld writes, "The typical reader will have read hundreds of stories and seen thousands of movies before beginning your story." This is a visionary scope. Of course, the reader comes to the page with their own library of associations, and there is no way that you can prepare for this. This will mean, of course, that some writers will be able to respond to your work, and others won't. This may relate to style or voice or content or form. It may or may not be a permanent condition for the reader. But knowing that the reader's participation includes everything she's seen or read is helpful advice for all writers. We need to remember that we are joining a huge collective knowledge in a reader's mind, and we need to know that it's all right if we don't eclipse every other book a reader has ever read. Our writing merely joins the reader's throngs of experiences.

Another source for mentoring is in your reading. E goes to JG Ballard for help with sentence-making and vocabulary, although he doesn't always love the books. He turns to Ursula LeGuin for her powerful capacity for world-building. S talks about Richard Margolis, who she grew up watching as a reader and writer in her childhood realm. He inspired her through his actions, and his writing, where he talked about difficult problems in an elegant and personable way. I have studied Russian novelists for their big-weaving of characters and psychological development. I have made friends with many contemporary writers, too, and I read their books for the double pleasure of their writing and the sense of reading a real, live person who is also breathing on this earth and translating their experiences into text. It gives me hope about writing more books myself, to see them doing it.

There are all kinds of anti-mentors who can mentor you, too. Years ago, I worked in a coffee shop and one of the regulars was an elderly Greek American man who had been a spy in World War II and then an artist during the beatnik and modernist birth in New York. He told wonderful stories, but we argued fiercely (usually when the cafe was closed, and I was washing counters and hauling out garbage). He claimed that there was no such thing as new art. That no new ideas were possible after the modernist movement. This went against every cell in my being. I believe in art's necessary role of responding to the changing world around us. Artists and writers and performers and musicians, all over the world, are doing vital work for humans, reflecting the world for us. Our world is constantly changing! I don't need those Madonna and child frescoes from Italy in 1550, for example, but somebody sure did. There are thousands of them. My world needs non-marginalized writing by queer people and by people of color, border stories and refugee stories. My world needs trans tv shows, novels told in tiny page-long segments, publications by writers of varied abilities, climate change artists, metoo movement art. Art moves change forward. It both pushes away and beckons. Our artists are observing for us, with their visual or auditory or linguistic or kinesthetic vessel. It's been twenty years since I knew that man, my anti-mentor, and I'm sure he's dead by now. Fighting with his limited perspective on those summer nights taught me who I am as an advocate and teacher and taught me what I believe about art and evolution of human societies.

We can invent anti-mentors, too. In *Still Writing*, Dani Shapiro writes that every writer has a shadow author. Someone whose book comes out at the same time, gets more press, has a more glamorous tour. In truth, we are only up against ourselves in these moments. We are being the enemy to our own success and light and pleasure. I envied a person with a good book deal. While I was on my own DIY book tour, my Envied Author posted a photo of themselves signing thousands of books at a big publishing house. Over the years, though, I found that even though Envied Author published in my genre of fabulism, I felt squeamish about Envied Author's work. I didn't really like it. Envied Author began posting boring notes about losing weight. I loathe discussions about weight. Envied Author mentioned all the things they were doing for their students. I was doing great things for my students, too. Would I want to be more like Envied Author? No. I wanted to be me, having some of the measure of success of Envied Author. But then didn't my jealousy obscure the fact that I did publish a book, that I did go on my own tour, that my small run of books had its own beloved readers? I was giving the joy away. So, I stopped following this person on social media (so easy!), and I made myself be grateful, instead, for what Envied Author did for others. By golly, I wished Envied Author well. And just like that, years went by when I didn't think of Envied Author. I don't even know where this author is, what they've published, what they teach. I've always been invisible to Envied Author, and now I can wish Envied Author well.

There are writing workshops full of anti-mentors, both who mean well and who don't. I was once in a writers' group where the leader always invited the most critical, insensitive participants to open the week's conversation on someone's story. From these bloody opening salvos, we worked our way back to some shred of praise, but I saw how reluctant people were to offer praise after the slaughter had begun. I suspected that the leader, who charged a fee for this group, was afraid the evening wouldn't be entertaining enough, so tossing chum into the waters was his way of guaranteeing a fun night. It became performance rather than real inquiry and discussion. I found that I didn't trust most of the writers in that group. At the end, there were only two people out of twelve whose advice I took into consideration, who, like me, refrained from entering the chum circle of peer humiliation. These writers offered their own, fresh responses to the work, free of any killer instinct. In this way, too, I was developing my own pedagogy as a writing mentor, assuming the role of guide, mentor, supporter, rather than judge or executioner, but more than that, I was teaching myself what kind of feedback would serve me and my writing.

The problem is that in some workshops, writers are allowed to use any old social model they've learned on the playground, at the cocktail party, at the sports arena, to scrabble themselves to an imagined top of the heap. A hierarchy is created to make one person seem strong and one person seem weak. I suggest we reject this paradigm of strong and weak, good and bad, winning or losing, in the world of feedback among writers. Any experienced writer will tell you that there is no heap, there is no top of the heap, there is no winning or losing. Buying into hierarchy creates an atmosphere of sadism in the workshop. Simultaneously, there is a belief among writers that only through suffering, hair shirts, and poisonous barbs, can we grow in our writing. This is what causes writers to willingly submit to the sadistic workshop, believing that this will help them become better writers. I am fervently against this dangerous belief system. There is plenty of difficulty and pain in a writing life. It doesn't have to come from our peers. It's as if everyone in a workshop has forgotten the power of words. The very tool we're trying to use to craft our texts, folks wield against each other in the work-shop without mercy. Constructive, communal-minded criticism can be observed and taught. The writing workshop should not be a shark tank, where the food is your newest most fragile ideas and sentences.

You can be a mentor for yourself, too. I know many writers who have been in particularly untended workshops and who have ended up spending a couple of years afterwards recovering emotionally before they can write again. This is certainly the fault of the instructors and programs, but we, as writers, should demand better, too. We need to advocate for our own safety in spaces where we're sharing new work, and to hell with the tradition, to hell with politeness. I have a saying, "Politeness will kill us in the end." I know it's hard to break with the tradition and culture of a classroom when you are a student. I suggest finding a peer you trust and creating a set of responses that you can rely on if the workshop isn't being carefully and thoughtfully moderated. It's vulnerable to be the one whose work is being discussed, so maybe your partner can raise a question in the workshop about objectivity and craft or some other redirection. If it's a particularly negative experience, maybe one of you accompanies the other out of the room. It's useful to learn to know when you are being defensive (though the advice is being offered is constructive) and when you are being harmed (because the advice being offered is an absolute or secretly self-oriented). Be creative and proactive and be on your own side.

It's wonderful to have readers. It's true magic to leap the divide between solitary thought and pen to having your ideas become shapes in another person's mind. Finding readers who like and need your work is sacred and exquisite. Feedback is not a meal that you must finish, though. Sometimes it is green-skinned potatoes and rancid nuts. Don't take crappy advice that goes against your gut. Learn the difference between what encourages you or what shuts you down or makes you feel defeated. Managing the responses takes careful listening, determined openness, and benevolent discipline. My friend, T, threw his workshop manuscripts away on his way out of the classroom building after a workshop. He'd heard what people had to say. He knew that the notes weren't going to help him because he knew himself. He knew he would obsess over them. He saved himself from that agony. You have permission to do whatever you want with any advice you get. You should be your most supportive mentor.

Create your own questions for readers to ponder and offer these with your text. Or ask for a specific kind of review where the reader looks exclusively at your structure, or exclusively at your characterizations, etc. If you know someone has a specific talent for certain kinds of feedback, ask them to focus on that. If you are feeling vulnerable about the work, tell the reader that. If someone is doing you the honor of giving you feedback, be sure that you honor your work, too, by telling the readers what you need.

If you've wanted to write and have looked to books on writing to help you, you'll know that some of these books are exciting and inspiring and some offer didactic, overly specific, or overly vague advice. *Always use third person. Never use third person. If there's no trauma, there's no suspense. Make the scene memorable.* Recently, a friend sent me a link for a "foolproof model for any text." Trust yourself. Does an approach appeal to you and make sense to you? Follow that advice. Does other advice that all your friends are following sound wrong to you? Don't follow that advice. Some advice-givers will even use phrases like, "The Final Word." Sometimes writers are advising me to write like they do, and the implication is that if I don't, I'm guaranteed to fail. Or worse, I'm already failing. The more I write, the more I know that a lot of writers' advice is good for them, good for many, but not necessarily for me. Not for everybody. Finding the advice that works for me is also a part of my writing work because we need different advice at different times, for different texts. There is no final word, friends. Please. Know this.

Of course, it's valuable that we read each other's work and offer our feedback, but this needs to be carefully offered and held to discussions of craft. People's dirty laundry of likes and dislikes needs to be dropped in trash bins by the door. Here are some examples of pointless, ignorant feedback that people have received in workshops.

- I'm so glad you don't have any incest in your story because I hate incest stories.
- As a white man, I can't relate to your Latinx character.
- I like your story because the exact same thing happened to me.
- No man would ever notice a baby's washcloth.
- This woman sounds Black, is she Black?
- I don't know any gay people, so I can't really speak to your story.
- I don't like violence, so I can't speak to this story.
- I don't like cities, so I can't speak to this story.
- I wish your story was funnier.
- Your characters are too cheesy.

E calls this the tyranny of "I," and you can see how the limitations are on the side of the reader. How could any of this ever be considered useful or allowed to stand by a workshop leader? There is plenty to discuss if you keep the conversation about craft. You can have a conversation on content, but this should be conducted with an eye to understanding the goal of the writer, not for the other writers to get on soapboxes and pontificate on a subject.

Tragically, I cannot count the number of students who have told me, "I had a teacher who told me I'm a terrible writer and that I should give it up." As readers, we must know the weight of our words, measure them, be responsible to our peers. Never tell someone they won't be any good, because the truth is, you don't know. People do incredible things. I'm sure that many people told the poet and essayist, Jimmy Santiago Baca, an orphaned kid on the streets who couldn't read or write, that he'd amount to nothing. Then he taught himself how to read and write in prison and went on to fill books and audience halls and start a literary non-profit. You don't know what people are capable of achieving. Furthermore, it's obvious that all of us are capable of achieving much more when we have people on our side.

There's another anti-mentor model in writing classes where peers are taught to say to each other about their newly written texts, *So what?* This makes me flinch. This is the language of playground bullying. "So what" means I don't care or it's not important. If I tell someone that I don't care, how will the writer get past this obstacle to try to reach me? This is a phrase that makes the recipient feel like they've already lost the game. Why not use a question that beckons more contemplation, such as, *And then what happened?* Or *What do you think is the most engaging line in this text?* Or *What do you think is the heart of this text? Do you think it's beating yet?*

If you believe that you should suffer at the hands of others to grow, you are your own anti-mentor. Once, early in a course, a student complained that the other members of the class didn't care about her work. I exclaimed, "What are you talking about? They really enjoy your work! They've all said so, pointing to things they specifically like!"

She said, "But they don't criticize it enough. No one has ever hurt my feelings."

This was a generative writing class. This student couldn't know that if she received a full criticism on work she'd written ten minutes previously, on a weekly basis, she would probably quit writing and never start again. There is a place for generation and encouragement, and a place for constructive suggestion. Her blanket belief that it should hurt or she wouldn't grow is a pervasive and sickening model. I roundly reject the belief that learning must hurt. Would anyone suggest that children with abusive parents have a better chance to grow? Why do we embrace a model that suggests an abusive environment helps a writer grow?

Do we need to be tortured to learn? Made to feel stupid or as though we are likely to fail? I use this example in my classrooms: when a baby is learning to walk, what do we say to baby? We say, *Come on, Sugar, you can do it! You're almost there! You're getting it!* We never say: *You're failing. That's a D-, dumb Baby!* We never say, *Don't quit your day job, Baby.* We say encouraging things and the baby tries and succeeds, and the baby tries and fails, and the baby tries and fails, and then the baby learns.

Let us, in the realm of writing generation and feedback, resist false hierarchy, false measurement, false comparison. Let us not crush each other with so whats. We can use plain old curiosity to get back to the essence. Felicia Rose Chavez has written a beautiful book, *The Anti-Racist Writing Workshop*, where she suggests authors offer statements and questions with their work, and readers are given suggestions for contemplative responses.

Social institutions must change as society changes. Reject old models of instruction or feedback that are meant to diminish you. Creative writing is as influenced by the patriarchy, English language standards, and white privilege as everything else in America, and the only way we can change it is by insisting on change in our own interactions.

One summer I had four different writer friends reading different texts and giving me feedback. After a few weeks of this, I felt overwhelmed, and then I remembered, Oh yes, everyone will always have something to say. They always will. So, you need to be the final voice, the final word. You are owner, parent, inventor. You need to be three stories tall, carrying your work out from the woods like the gift that it is.

Do you feel like writing?

Do you have someone who hovers over your writing life like an evil overlord, condemning you before you write your first word? Turn this anti-mentor into an archetypal villain. Use aspects that you know about them to include in the description (cotton stuffed in the ears, high-water pants, long-nose hairs, a musty smell?), and describe them doing something deceitful or mischievous or dangerous. As writers we have power. Make your anti-mentors small.

Do you feel like writing?

Pay attention to how a club or class or group of friends works. If you can, take notes at a meeting or a practice or gathering. Who leads? Who hides? Who is checked out? Who elongates the meeting? Who talks about something that probably should be between them and the leader only, or them and one other person? When are you engaged? When are you bored? Do you know why you are there? What is the general tone of the meeting and who sets it? Who is the first to leave? Who is the last to leave? Do you want to be there? Practice thinking about how a group works and think about what you might want in one. How do you advocate for your own needs or desires, or do you? Observing your own interactions with community and looking critically at what you like or dislike will help you know what you want in a writing community. Once you know this, think about inviting one or two people to either write with you, or to talk about writing, or to share and discuss writing. I suggest starting small, because we don't always have the managerial skills needed to make a larger group work.

Do you feel like writing?

Find mentors. Make an enormous list of influences. List every musician, poet, writer, artist, performance artist, activist, figure in history that you can think of who has influenced you, or name every speech, drawing, poem, story created or lived by those people. Are there any commonalities in content/delivery/tone/philosophy/style? Try and pinpoint the aspects of the people or the work that move you, so that you have a strong sense of how you are motivated.

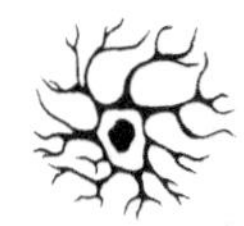

CHAPTER ELEVEN

Art Bears Truths

Did this really happen?

Students in my fiction classes often asked this of each other at the beginning of the course. As if a real story is better than the one that exists on the page, that this "realness" would somehow be more authentic, more precise. Fiction is a truth-teller, though. A fiction writer may shape-shift with craft, but the truth hovers up and out of this new form, offering a kind of revealing fictional light that slices through the murk of half-remembered or reconstituted detail to reveal a new perspective, an emotional truth, something previously unconsidered.

It's a hard era for truth, but art bears truths.

Once I was enduring an awful grief and the only way that I could manage getting through a day of the agony was to write a paragraph, at least a paragraph, a day. I would conjure one image or imagined conversation or clarified moment that represented my suffering and write it down. A novella grew out of this daily gathering of paragraphs. The experiences of grief were transformed into visceral, violent, bodily articulations. The narrator cuts off her tongue. Her head falls off and rolls away. A bone slides off into the dark. The narrator jams fish spines in her throat and tries to dance. A fat little monster moves into the house. These are metaphorical devices. Regardless, every detail felt extremely personal, and when I began submitting it, I submitted it as non-fiction. I told my friend, S, about a non-fiction contest I'd sent it to, and she looked startled.

"What?" I asked. "You don't think it's non-fiction? It's completely autobiographical, though!"

"Are you sure?" S asked, cocking her head at me.

I looked into her blue eyes, which looked mildly concerned, and I started laughing. "Oh," I said. "I guess my head didn't really fall off, did it? Is that what you mean?"

"Yes," she said, relieved. "That's what I mean."

My fictive mind and my real-life mind blend. My concept of reality has always been flexible, which perhaps explains why fiction is my main genre. This started early. When I walked into the classroom in second grade, I thought that maybe I was still in first grade and only dreaming that I was in second grade. I never assume that there is only one reality. Because of this, my real-life mind uses the images that my imagination provides as ways to comprehend what has happened. Plain facts of a story don't always correctly illustrate the massive, shifting nature of experience.

Our most precise memories, in fact, are flush with fat inventions and this leaves us with different kinds of *truth*. Every memory is recreated. It is a notorious fact that people often get details wrong in police reports. I caught a burglar in my house one winter, and a police officer asked me, "Was he wearing gloves?"

"Yes." And then I said, "No. I have no idea. I can't remember his hands at all." I stood five feet away and watched him get on his bike and ride away. You would think that I would have known if he was wearing gloves. But I wasn't even looking at him, in some way. I wanted to know that my cat and my computer were okay, so I missed the pertinent details. I'm a writer. I'm observant. I have a good memory. Everything is about details for me. But was he wearing gloves? No idea.

The trouble of this witness is neurological. In *The Brain: The Story of You,* David Eagleman writes, "what we experience as seeing relies less on the light streaming into our eyes and more on what's already inside our heads." He goes further in this book to note: "The meaning of something to you is all about your webs of associations, based on the whole history of your experiences... You don't perceive objects as they are. You perceive them as you are." Our brains are always filtering, always casting experiences in a certain light. Therefore, we miss details, perhaps, but also a reason to rely on our fifth brains in writing. The fifth brain is a constant weaver of meaning and importance.

This is not simply a theoretical idea, that we invent our stories, whether fiction or memory. From a study reported in *Atlantic Monthly,* UC Irvine's Center for the Neurobiology of Learning's professor James McGaugh explains "that memory is colored with bits of life experiences. When people recall, 'they are reconstructing,' he said. 'It doesn't mean it's totally false. It means that they're telling a story about themselves and they're integrating things they really do remember in detail, with things that are generally true.'" But what are the "things that are generally true"? Integration of "bits of" experience and general truths don't sound as solid a foundation of truth as we'd like to believe. "Reconstructing" sounds a lot like writing. Integrating details to create a story. Even if a story isn't directly about the writer or the writer's experiences, it reveals what the writer notices, what the writer is interested in, or curious about. We're always constructing and reconstructing from our own specific brain platform.

From the same study, Elizabeth Loftus reports, "It's so powerful when somebody tells you something and they have a lot of detail. . . Especially when they express emotion. To just say, 'Oh my god it must be true.' But all those characteristics are also true of false memories, particularly the heavily rehearsed ones that you ruminate over. They can be very detailed. You can be confident. You can be emotional. So, you need independent corroboration.'" Emotional memories, false memories, rehearsed memories. It's uncomfortable to admit, to know, that memory can be so flawed. That truth is only achievable through independent corroboration.

What is fiction and what is truth? Who bears the *absolute* truth? Politicians and first responders are learning the power of digital eyewitness. Even then, people can manipulate the order of images, pretend to lose the images. The use of untampered cellphone video has become vital to record the harassment of Black, Indigenous and people of color by the police. That "independent corroboration" has been vital in bringing awareness to the rampant racism in a country that wants to pretend that racism is over. In fact, in this computer age, we are surrounded by truths being cast as fiction and fictions being cast as real events. When I began writing this book, ChatGPT didn't exist. A world where a program can mimic human writing well is an unrecognizable world. But ChatGPT is never going to have a fifth brain.

The ten billion shapers of history in various countries have specialized in blurring the line between "truth" and "corroborated" truth for reasons of power or control or tradition. North Koreans were told that their previous leaders didn't defecate. For thousands of years, the Chinese believed that small feet were a mark of beauty and thus induced billions of female children into the torture of foot binding. As recently as 2016, a textbook ordered for schools in the state of Texas describes ships full of slaves as ships full of *laborers*. The teller can cast a tale in any light.

Truth is a kind of holy grail, rumored and dreamt of and rarer than we want to acknowledge. This is daunting, when we're talking about history, but when we're talking about fiction, it's a vast, clear space of possibility simply waiting for the writer. All knowledge is shaped or integrated or punctuated truth. There is room here for a writer to tell their tale.

Still, writing experiences into fiction is a way to speak of human truths. I propose that imagination is another kind of corroboration. Using your imagination to find the through-line of symbol or intention in a story can lead to a story that feels more authentic than a mere recitation of events might. My suggestion here is both simple and complex. You have to let the experienced story change inside of you so that you can write a "truer" story. You are the one who knows what "really happened," and you can lift the parts that seem essential, but it's best to relinquish devotion to the chronology, geography, attendance of the real event. When my then-boyfriend had a brain tumor, I wrote a short story about a modern plague that overtakes a couple's house. The woman allows a stray cat in the house. The cat carries the fleas that bring the plague, and the husband blames his wife for their predicament. They endure medical procedures, fear, and confusing reports of a kind of plague-ghoul. I was using the plague as a metaphor for the cancer that had entered our lives, and I wanted to describe the different ways that my boyfriend and I responded to the devastating events. The narrator becomes feverishly creative, and the husband retracts and grows silent. In real life, I selected elements from the true story. There was a stray cat, there were strange medical interactions, and there was a sense that a monster had been let loose in our house. The story ends with the couple reclaiming their lives despite the devastating circumstances, and this is what the truth of that time taught me, that all your life (the good and the bad) is your only life and that you need to choose how to live it. I let my imagination corroborate the psychological essence of a story and then I see what happens on the page.

Sometimes writers pretend that writing isn't mysterious. But we make marks on a page and then a kind of magic occurs when another person (maybe a stranger) reads these marks and our thoughts bloom in their imagination. Sometimes we forget that magic that happens in the writer, too. Among the mysteries of writing, the truth is that writing can develop and succor us as humans, can lead us into our most authentic selves. Once I had a radical writing vision at a concert. I'd seen something upsetting, but I didn't want to leave the concert. I listened to the music, secretly panicking although I kept my face expressionless. After a while, I felt a breeze and turned back to look at the entrance of the venue. Characters from my first novel were strolling in through the doors of the theatre, each one of them ten feet tall, wearing the ragged clothing of settlers, and smelling of the ocean. I couldn't have been more surprised. Such presence! In that instant, I grew in confidence and love and self-reliance. The real people who upset me are temporary flashes in my life's journey, but what I've written is mine, forever. There is little else in life that a person can own so completely as their imagination. Did this really happen to me? Or was it a vision? Yes. Yes.

Literature offers us different ways to be human, to live through the impossible moments that we are going to have to live through. For writers, reinventing an impossible experience in fiction can give you power over something you feel that you have no power over. We can write about what is real in the human experience, even if it's fictionalized. The essence of what it is to be human is not written on hallmark cards or found in the fiction of Hollywood movies where everything works out beautifully. Happily ever afters are not possible, perhaps, in a world where everyone dies. The truth of human existence is much messier, crunchier, and riddled with difficulties. One of our choices as writers is selecting the truths that are valuable to us to explore, things that will help us navigate this life.

We will meet difficulty, but should we be any less attentive, any less alive, any less our writer selves even in that difficulty? I am suggesting that when we are stripped of our illusions of safety and complacency, that we find ourselves at the height of living. That discomfort is the real story. It's the truth underneath our casseroles and schedules and uniforms and retirement plans, that the lives we live are mostly mystery. There's a truth we want to reject and yet it remains.

When I became serious about writing fiction in my twenties, I became friends with a night clerk in a crappy seaside hotel. He had the night shift after mine and showed up, either showered and holding a big cup of soda, two books, and a pack of cigarettes, or he showed up drunk and disheveled with a big cup of whiskey and a crumpled pack of cigarettes. One night he showed up with a copy of Tim O'Brien's *The Things They Carried,* telling me, "I think you are a person who will like this book." When I opened the book, it smelled terrible, like mold and vomit and cigarettes, but I stayed up all night reading. He was right. Not only do I like this book, but it revealed the slippery nature of truth.

In this book, O'Brien has a story titled "How to Tell a True War Story," which repeats the phrase "a true war story" over and over in different variations. I studied this story again and again, while I was learning to trust the truth of my own fictional worlds. O'Brien's lines illustrate the ways that he simply points to the impossibility of knowing a *final truth.* The relentless reframing of this idea is like a hammer, seeming to crack at something impenetrable and unyielding, although the use of craft in repetition and variation inevitably reveals truths about war.

"A true war story is never moral."

"You can tell a true war story if it embarrasses you."

"In any war story, but especially a true one, it's difficult to separate what happened from what seemed to happen. What seems to happen becomes its own happening and has to be told that way."

"In many cases, a true war story cannot be believed."

O'Brien notes that war stories are immoral, embarrassing, happening, unbelievable, untellable, unending, meaningful, specific, and felt. Writing about difficult things might require other ways of telling. Metaphors, repetitions, retelling. O'Brien opens and closes circuits of logic about truth, about war, as the story builds, using language to illustrate the limitations of language in the face of horror.

Fictive imagination is a place of considerable power. There is breadth and potential for negative influence, too. In his book,

Fearless Writing, William Kenower warns us that there are dangers to imagination. He reminds us that our imagination will go anywhere we allow it to, and we should be careful to identify the unhelpful paths we tread. I know people who can imagine the worst outcome for any event. Car accidents, flu, cancer, diabetes. These people *always* imagine the call in the middle of the night. (This is trauma, of course. Once you have gotten a call with bad news, it's hard to forget that it can happen.) But the danger is that our imaginations will go there easily, entirely, all in. We can become obsessed with the horrors that our imaginations create for us. We use the same part of our brain to imagine our own deaths as we do to build a world in fiction. Kenower reminds us that we can pull back! Whew! We can go eat barbecue on buns or chickpeas or drink coffee and let that vision go. It's key to be aware of this as you intentionally develop your imagination.

Fictive power is positive and generative and endless. We have the power to give our good memories to our texts and characters. Here's a memory: I'm staring down at a host of fiddler crabs on the banks of an inlet in Sunset Beach, South Carolina. There is black and green mud. The fat claws rise in unison against me, the water laps next to us, there is the unmistakable stink of a fecund inlet bank. I was eight or nine years old, and I couldn't stop staring at them with delight. Here it is as fiction, where I've given it to a character in my novel, *Origin*: "The women were in conversation and forgot to nag Liny to keep up. He let them walk ahead and he crouched quietly by the marshy banks, watching as the fiddler crabs rose from their defensive positions and went back to gathering mud in fat clods. He was absorbed in this, in the heft of their bodies, in the mass of their color, when a large fish jumped, sounding a huge slap, and Liny watched ring after ring after ring of the early morning blue spiraling across the water." Those fiddler crabs are as real for Liny Leggith as they are for me. Now they are memory *and* fiction. They have become double imagination vectors! I own two worlds at once.

Do you feel like writing?

Here is a prompt to practice fictionalizing experiences. Take an intense memory. Recast the same memory in a different way (change setting, character, year). Write it. Next, recast it again in yet a different way (change setting, character, year a second time) and write it again. What are the throughlines that you need to keep? What is flexible?

Do you feel like writing?

Write a true "war" story. (This could be real war on tv, as a refugee, militarization, or in your life experience, or other kinds of embattlements, such as divorce, addiction, mental illness, etc.)

CHAPTER TWELVE

For the Love of Writing

- Name the best painting on earth.
- Name the best book ever written.
- Name the best art form.
- Name the best genre of writing.
- The best artist?
- The best writer?

We operate as if such truths exist. Do you believe such truths exist? If you ask five friends to answer the questions above, do you think they will have the same answers?

There are useful hierarchies in structures that help them function in nature (skeletal, circulatory, respiratory), in the natural order of animals (alpha male gorillas), in human families (parents and young children), and in the organization of businesses where someone is accountable for the success of the other parts (board of directors, CEO, advisory board). There are books written about these structures and their benefits and failures, but I am not discussing these. I am discussing what happens when hierarchical structures are inappropriately applied to creative endeavors. I am talking about the Falsehood of Artistic Hierarchy!

Hierarchies in art and writing are invented. We have best seller lists, awards, contests, winners, and losers galore. In the artistic milieu, these are ways we show our appreciation. They are not, as often perceived, a hierarchical fact of authority or divinity bestowing "best-ness." After all, who among us is knowledgeable and visionary enough to make these distinctions?

As an undergrad, I remember an evening with other writing students, settled on mismatched couches in a rented house, drinking cheap beers and discussing authorial context. *Should you read works with knowledge of their author's life or not?* No one could agree. People were fiercely on one side or the other. I watched the others make their arguments and wondered how we had each arrived at our conclusions, since we were at the same small college, taking a lot of the same classes with the same professors. Each of us had opinions, and I had a flash of intuition about how many experiences, readings, conversations, thoughts, teachings, and personalities it had taken for each of us to come to our conclusion. My own certainties (that people should let texts stand for themselves) crumbled in the face of so many interesting points of view.

Imagine the infinite differences between writers in financial, geographic, cultural, spiritual, emotional, physical circumstances. Imagine the ways that these differences lead to an infinite number of texts. Imagine trying to rank every book in the world. Imagine trying to rank every book in the world knowing that you haven't and won't ever see them all.

Additionally, let's imagine the rankers. What is their racial profile, economic status, level of education, level of privilege, level of emotional stability, level of knowledge of texts in the world, level of support in their lives? Are they aware of their own preferences in style or voice or content? Do you trust all of them to set these aside for a fair and impartial judgment? The problem is that those who judge, award, deem "bestness" are themselves a sea of variations. In a country struggling with severe and endless inequities it is certain that many exquisitely talented, nuanced, original, necessary voices go unheard.

I don't even know the "best" of my own work. I have stories that I like more than others but when I ask readers what they like best, they invariably name different pieces! I love all of my texts for the different parts of me they reveal, for the ways that the writing taught me something I didn't understand, for the characters who came and shared their struggles and their wisdom. I am grown by every text I write. Ranking them seems an impossible, pointless endeavor.

Trying to publish means wrestling with hierarchy. If you are interested in sharing your work with others, finding publication for it, then you understand that rejection is a part of the writing game and this is why it is important to be clear about who is on your side (you), and why it is important to remember that the whole publishing game (a complex hierarchy of perceptions) is created and inhabited and enacted by fallible humans just like us. (If you are not interested in sharing your work, then please love it for all the reasons you love it and ignore the rest of this chapter.)

When I started sending submissions out, I used the classified section of print editions of *Poets and Writers Magazine*. That magazine was new, and the internet was only a fledgling, and I was an emerging writer in the Outer Banks of North Carolina, taking care of my grandfather who was suffering from dementia. He watched reruns of *CHIPS* and *Bonanza* while I wrote my awkward first stories in his study and my boyfriend listened to baseball in the guest bedroom. In the early 90s, you sent submissions in brown clasp envelopes with postage-paid, self-addressed letter envelopes inside to receive your rejection or acceptance. I kept a notebook where I stapled the rejections that came with the returned manuscripts. Sometimes the rejections had little handwritten notes on them, once a drawing of a tree. The notebook got fat. I learned that the work of submissions is never in vain because you learn, publication by publication, what kind of writing is out there, what kinds of journals, what kinds of presses, what kinds of publishers, what kinds of contests, what kinds of readers there are. All the understandings and knowledge of a writer build and build and build, in both internal and external ways. Nothing is wasted. Patience is necessary.

Submissions have gotten a lot more efficient and less personal over the years with Submittable, including template-style rejections and acceptances, so it's an even more necessary practice to enjoy the work of researching journals or presses or agents, reading the work they publish, or reading about who they are. Trust that this work accrues into knowledge of your field. Once I submit a text, I "sip on a can of maybe" for as long as it takes to hear back. Sometimes I get published. Sometimes I don't. I still love these places that honor reading and writing, whether they publish my work. I'm still rooting for them and I'm still rooting for my work. I believe in relishing the power of ownership over your own texts. Your texts don't exist to be rejected or accepted. They exist because you had something to say. It's this that keeps me alive in a long history of writing and submissions, learning what it is that I have to say in this life and owning it.

Being a curious person saves me. I like to imagine editors at their desks. Writing students choosing work for their university literary magazine. Agents walking through the offices where their pictures are taken for the agency's webpage. I wonder what these people's lunches are like, what frustrations they've had that day, what they are hoping will happen for a book or literary journal or in their own daily lives. My curiosity gives me room to take rejections with a grain of salt. These are ordinary people, making the decisions. People having good days and bad days and anxiety attacks and indigestion and arguments with their spouses or getting raises or planning special dinners. Also, these people have all kinds of different tastes in writing styles and genres. Remember that not all rejections or acceptances are equal, either. It takes a great measure of wisdom and self-awareness to learn to appreciate work that doesn't personally appeal to you, and I am sure that some of the folks doing the selection aren't this self-aware. It can be helpful to know that you're not always being rejected or even accepted by someone whose opinion you would admire if you knew them.

Ultimately, you don't need to believe that a rejection, or the people deciding not to publish your writing, are correct. The hierarchies inherent in ideas of success or failure are consensual contracts whether we realize it or not, and you don't have to consent to them to do your writing. You can *reject a rejection* and continue to believe in your own work.

The act of "getting published" is much quieter than I'd imagined. The first time I got an acceptance, there was a phone call with an editor on the line, telling me that I'd won the *Philadelphia Weekly* Fiction Contest, that my story would be published with an illustration, I'd get to read it for an audience, and I'd receive a check for $350 dollars. I was elated. In truth, the piece came out and it was cool, and the money was spent and then time went on. I thought there would be something more, some feeling of belonging to the "real world" of writing.

I needn't have worried. There is no "real world" of writing. Just countless other writers writing, thinking, teaching, making a living, publishing, editing, rejecting, and reading each other. Some make money at it, but many do not. Some are arrogant, some are humble. Some live in Los Angeles, some in Topeka, some in France, Argentina, China. They have partners or kids or pets. Their parents are living or dead. Some are lonely and some are thrilled and some are addicted. Some are reading books and some are digging gardens and some are eating cupcakes and some are buying yoga pants and some are getting a little rejection *ding!* in their email box right now.

Occasionally, I go to a bookstore to see the thousands of titles and thousands of authors. I am aware that I am in only one bookstore in one town in one country, largely in one language. There are zillions of other bookstores with books in other languages, and books in the ether, and books in our homes and books in our minds. When I go to a bookstore, I am reminded that there is room for me. There is always more room. You can contribute significantly to this treasure if you so desire. If you are a writer who wants to write, if you have something to say, then feel free to do the work of sharing it, too.

Sometimes writers are jealous and resentful when other people they know publish or receive opportunities. I have seen this many times and I urge you to resist this poison. Those bitter worms of jealousy can writhe and ruin any good day. It's as if the success steals something we think should be ours, or as if someone else's success threatens what we desire. This response makes us feel small and mean and bereft. The word "compersion" is not in English dictionaries yet, but it's a word popular in polyamory communities meaning being *delighted on someone else's behalf.* I have found that resisting jealousy and practicing compersion offers the benefit of more joy. It's simple. I make a choice to experience vicarious joy instead of vicarious pain. It's a practice that you can learn, and the rewards are tremendous. It keeps us from being self-absorbed and allows us to engage in and feel real pleasure.

I suggest a steady diet of celebration and congratulations. Accomplishments in a creative life can be quiet. It's hard to explain how intense it can feel to finish a draft. It's usually just you, alone in a room with your own sentences. So, if someone you know finishes a draft of something and mentions it, celebrate it with them. If someone you know finishes a book, celebrate it with them. If someone you know publishes something, celebrate it with them! Find a way that feels comfortable, maybe post your celebration on social media, or write them a note of congratulations, or offer to have a celebration over a sweet treat (in person or over the computer). It's easy and it feels good, and it builds community.

A writer must be true to their own goals and dreams. Comparing ourselves to others can feed an airless, purposeless narrative of our own failure. There's no room to grow if you have already failed, if you believe there is no room for you. The chances are high that we are wrongly imagining the perfection of another's situation, or that we're misinformed. Name one person who doesn't have some struggle in their lives sooner or later. The human condition has plenty of difficulties to go around and many of the hardships are invisible.

There is such a thing as benign envy, which is different. This is a kind of envy that might drive us towards bigger risks, things we might not try if we didn't witness someone else having readings, publishing a book, teaching, writing a beautiful sentence or line. It's a muscular act, to keep ourselves out of the pit of self-pity and bitterness, to keep ourselves in a beneficent realm where we think: why not me, too? Any muscle will build with repetitive use. Our determination needs to be built, too. We could build a self-pity muscle just as easily as a determined, optimistic muscle, but it is a choice. How do you want to feel about your writing life?

There's another intangible hardship of not getting published. *The witnesses.* If you have a community, friends, and family that you're in touch with, it can be hard to struggle in front of these witnesses. It can be embarrassing to have them worry over you. While I was writing this, I got an agent's rejection for a novel that I really hoped would be a good match for her. It's kind of a heartbreaking situation for me, this novel. It has fans who have read it multiple times for their own pleasure. It's had (and lost) agent interest over the years. With every rejection, I'm at the crossroads again. One agent commented on my affection for the characters. I thought: *Is that bad? Should I hide that affection?* An ex once scoffed that I should stop celebrating each revision of the novel. I thought: *Should I mourn it instead? Should I bury it?* Sometimes I pretend I'm going to stop sending it out, so that I don't seem crazy. But I'm probably not going to stop. I love this novel, and that big giant blue eye of my three-story self is always behind me, whispering, *Let's try again.*

I don't want to give up on this book, so I will celebrate it. Should I mourn that I keep revising a novel that I haven't gotten published but love too much to put away? Would that be good for me? What are we to do with our actual feelings about the works we want to publish and haven't yet? If it's love, as I propose, the relationship between myself and my work, then all I can do is love it, celebrate it, and defend my right to love it. Giving up on it would gouge a hole in my heart. There is mystery here, too. Perhaps submitting this book is a ritual practice that is vital to all my other writing. I am willing to believe that I might not know why it's important for me to keep this book alive, but that it is meaningful all the same.

For years before I published a book, I participated in readings, organized readings for others, attended open mics. I love the circles of sharing work. I want to behold how another person writes or reads. I love performing my own work. I love having people inside my work with me. I love talking about the alchemy of language and content and reader. Ever since the first time that I tried to write a scene so that someone who wasn't there could experience it someday, I was hooked. For me, it's always been about the someday interaction of translating the world that I see for another person. It's no mistake that the word "love" appears five times in this paragraph. Sharing work is an invitation, a beckoning into imagination, a scene, a moment, a concept, an understanding. Sharing your work indicates a belief in the human capacity that a stranger can understand and appreciate the way your imagination works. Sharing your work is a form of love.

When my short story collection came out and got a favorable review in *Publisher's Weekly*, the small press publisher called and told me, "You've got it made!" I was thrilled and walked around my small desert house with my book clutched in my hand. I remember staring at the orange Saltillo tile floor and asking myself, "*Have* I got it made?" There was a finality to the phrase that didn't resonate with me. I did "have it made" in that I published my first book. I got a positive review! I experienced the uncanny, breathtaking experience of readers connecting with my ideas and reflecting my themes and language and content back to me, which helped me continue to grow as a writer and a thinker. Eventually, I realized that "having it made" means celebrating my relationship with writing, the privacy of my imagination, and engaging with these aspects of my own life often and forever.

Everyone has an opinion about writing. When I was visiting Cyprus, I met a flirtatious olive farmer who told me that I needed to write a mystery, or a romance, and sell it, and then I could write anything I wanted. Next, he advised me that good writing, the best writing, must come from the marrow. He said that only this writing gets published. Also, he advised me that every book you write must be the very best you can write, and then it would automatically sell. I stared at him, knowing that he was giving me conflicting, ignorant advice. This was a poor flirting technique. I would never have tried to give him advice on growing olives. I knew that what he was saying was that he didn't know the first damn thing about writing. I knew that he was saying out loud things that lots of people have said before or thought or think. I took a sip from the glass of wine in front of me and didn't correct him. I felt too tired, in fact, to correct him. In some ways, he'd outlined the terrible situation. First, some mysteries and romances might "come from the marrow." Writing from "the marrow" doesn't mean that your books will sell, regardless of genre. Also, I couldn't bear defending all my books as the best thing I could write because then wouldn't that imply that my best wasn't enough because they haven't all been published? There was little point in explaining the complexities of the digital age of publishing, the systems of presses, agents, journals, writing programs, equity, best sellers vs. back titles vs. titles out of print. But it would be easy to get sucker-punched in such a conversation, in such limited ideas of success and failure. I didn't even bother to convince him of what I know for sure: that my continued writing is the real success, and the only one that I can control.

I love my stories. I love to write. I love to read. I love to be read, to give my texts the gift of coming alive in a stranger's imagination. That fierce love and empowerment motivates this book. You can grant yourself permission to feel this way about your own writing. No hierarchy has given me permission to say this to you but as I sometimes say in conversation when I know exactly where a writer is stuck, *I promise you, I'm right about this.* What happens next (and then next after that and after that) in your writing life is up to you. Go ahead and write.

Do you feel like writing?

Write two letters of submission for something you've written or something you want to write. Make one formal, following all the rules of submission stated by a journal you like. Then write a second a letter. Fill it with typos, a wacky font, break all the rules of proper submission. Say intimate things about your life. Tell them who you wish your writing was like in the most arrogant of ways: I am the next Gabriel Garcia Marquez, bitches! If you get into the work of submitting, you'll have plenty of chances to wince over typos or little things you thought you caught but you didn't. So, break all the rules, just once, for fun.

Do you feel like writing?

Luckily, "having it made" looks like sitting in my study at the computer, writing, birds and squirrels or lizards fluttering or scampering or scaling past my window, the whole day stretched into hours of reading and writing and exercise and when I stop writing, wandering into the kitchen and pouring the leftover writing mind and heart into a recipe, pulling down pots and cranking up the oven, slicing and chopping and salting and searing.

What does having it made look like for you?

Do you feel like writing?

Write about someone that you envy. Make up two stories about their daily lives, one that is full of delight and success and one that is terrible. Remember that you are a writer, and you have power in this world to create outcomes.

CHAPTER THIRTEEN

Do You Feel Like Writing?

A Chapter of Prompts

These are prompts for you to play with. The list is broken into sections loosely titled by their origination or their goal: Imagination, Character, Self-portrait, and Craft Techniques. There is no way of doing these exercises incorrectly. Trust your fifth brain to take you where you need to go and remember that all prompts can be altered to address qualities of the writer or a character or text as needed.

Imagination

- Turn a person from your life into an archetypal character, such as a witch, goblin, king, warrior, princess, monster, troll, oracle, goddess, etc.

- Think about an animal that has qualities like a character you are working with and write a paragraph or two using language from that animal's habitat or description or use as a symbol to help illustrate your character. You can look up pictures/descriptions of an animal to help you with the language. (If you have a bullying, blunt character, perhaps you use the language of a bull: horns, broad shoulders, glossy black hide, virility, strength.)

- Write a story about a group (family, travelers, friends, coworkers) that is at a crossroads (literally or figuratively). What do they see as their choices? Do they agree on their choices? What is at stake? What does each member of the group want?

- Write an etiological tale that explains the existence of rain, fire, ocean, human murder, redemption, the color of the sky, psychology, domesticated pets, or sin.

- Think of metaphorical or real plagues you are aware of in the modern human condition and begin a story where this plague takes over or write a scene for the middle of it. (This can be metaphorical or biological, such as Plague of Cell phone usage, Ebola, Plague of Denial, Avian flu, use of straws, Swine Flu, Plague of foodie-ism, Bubonic Plague, Plague of Locusts, Pneumonic Plague, Plague of Weed Dispensaries, Plague of Surveys, or your own invented plague.)

- Write a letter response to a fictional letter the narrator has received. Use quotes from the letter, but never directly address the relationship between the two authors.

- Tell a story using a phone conversation as the framework. Something is burning.

- A partner demands an explanation from their partner about adulteries. The accused responds with a series of small stories.

- Draw a portrait of a character using only a series of their daydreams.

- Find a seeker in your work.

- Write about the shadows of a place. (Ghosts, moods, literal shadows, history, etc.)

- Find something on a science website and journal. Choose one participant, either scientist or animal or star or germ and write about the science from this point of view.

- Furniture and household items are often full of story. What catches your eye every time you walk through a particular house? A green couch with mahogany feet. A green-blue print on the wall. A mousetrap. The little statues on the mantel. Any object could be the subject of a poem, an essay, or as a symbol in a story.

- Describe the intellectual, physical, emotional, spiritual life of a mountain, a bar at night, a city street, a church, etc.

Character

- Describe a terrible moment in a character's life. Write in present tense to make it seem to the reader that it is happening right now. (Break up? Caught in a lie? Abandoned? Imprisoned? Stranded?)

- Write a scene where a character is remembering something/ someone in their life that has been ruined.

- Write a story where a character realizes that something they believed about themselves absolutely isn't true.

- Write a character explaining *Why I did what I did.*

- Create a heap of memories for a character to discover interesting parts of their history. Tricking your brain with a repeated phrase can distract you enough to let all sorts of interesting details slide out of your brain. Beginning with something like "she remembers," "they remember," or "I remember," and list fifteen memories. Let them come from imagination or life. Do not block them with value judgments. Just let them arrive and scribble them down. Then choose the most interesting one and expand into a story or use the repeated line throughout the story if you like.

- Create a character who is not the same race, gender, or cultural background as you. Research and read articles and essays written by people who are of this race, gender, sexual identity, or cultural background to make this character expand beyond a stereotype. What is at stake for this character?

- Write the thoughts of a character at school or work, interspersed with their daydreams.

- Write about a character who has arrived in a completely new place. Show them either learning to accept the new place or show them fighting everything about the new place. This place could be a town, city, state, country, planet.

- A character slips into a funeral uninvited.

- Write from the point of view of a character who feels trapped, either psychologically or physically.

- Write about a character who is cooking or building something while they work a relationship problem out in their minds.

- Have one character play a practical joke on another character. Does the joke go over well? Does the joke incite a fight?

- Write a character who cannot fit into a group they want to fit into.

- Write a story where something is stolen. Play with what this might be (Object? Identity? Innocence? Hair? A wooden leg? A whole house?)

- Write about a character who strives to be perfectly honest.

- Each person has some experience, some quirk, some shadow or light that makes them like no other. Let your characters show themselves to you. For example, on a train into

Amsterdam I met a woman from Liverpool. She wore poorly attached false eyelashes, a little black decorative elastic band around her neck that she tugged at. Her shirt was hot pink, and her Liverpool accent was thick and delicious. She'd been drinking, she told me, two gins on the plane and two beers at the airport, and she was headed for a canal booze cruise with some friends. When she showed me a picture of her gap-toothed, pig-tailed daughter, I knew the child's name was Phoebe from a tattoo on the woman's wrist, which I saw again and again as she tugged at her elastic choker. This woman's ebullience was infectious, and even though I saw other people in our train car glancing at us in annoyance, I let her teach me her Liverpool accent. We practically shouted "A*maz*ing!" and "Where you *been*?" and we laughed at the nothingness of it. She offered to come write a book with me, and we compared arms so that she could show me how she needs a tan, and she hugged me when we parted. "You'll remember old Carly," she told me. I do. I do remember Carly. Choose a person and show us the minutiae of their actions as they do something characteristic unto themselves.

- Examine your knowledge of terms. I know writing terms, cooking terms, and teaching terms. I have friends who know divination and hoodoo terms. I know people who have economist language. Make a list of your own sets of terms and start writing a story with a character who is similarly equipped.

- Write about a character who thinks she is dead, or near death. Don't dwell on wounds or illness or accident. What details, memories, or fantasies emerge in the character's mind?

- Write a story from an "other voice" point of view such as rain, fire, smoke, earthquake, tidal wave, snow, clouds. Write out what this thing sees or thinks or says.

- If you are struggling with a character, go into their closet and see what kinds of shoes, shirts, accessories they have. See how they keep their closet. Is it messy or pristinely organized? Let some of their belongings show you something you didn't know about them.

- Think of a character you dislike in someone else's work. Describe why you don't like them.

- Make a playlist for a character.

- From whence does once of your characters derive their spirit, drive, or personality?

- What does a character dream for their future, or do they live in the moment only?

- Does your character face the present, past, future, or all three at once? What are the problems this presents for them? What are the strengths?

- What subject makes your character feel hopeless?

- What feels out of control in the personality of one of your characters?

- Show us a character on a day when they are completely alone and bummed out. Where are they? What do they think about? What repeats? What gets out of proportion? Do they call someone? Do they go somewhere? Do they put on music?

- Identify the character you've written who mostly closely resembles you. What are this character's flaws and strengths?

- Write a list of a character's former love interests with just a sentence about each.

- Look at the identities the characters in your texts. Make a list of your important characters. Are there variations in racial identity, sexual identity, levels of economics? Do they have any physical, mental, or emotional divergences? Are they all the same? How are they different?

- Write the birth or death scene for one of your characters, regardless of whether it would ever appear in your text. Think about characterization, setting, dialogue, internal monologue, magic, ordinariness, pacing.

- Think about one of your characters that is guarded or one that lacks boundaries. How does this person protect/not protect their beliefs? How does this person protect/not protect their knowledge? How does this person protect/not protect their emotions? How does this person protect/not protect their hungers or yearning? Is anyone able to protect themselves?

- Write a scene from one of your own experiences of being lost. Write down every bit of the detail you can remember. Time of day? Location? Who were you with? What was the weather? Were you alone or with others? What are your immediate reactions to being lost? Do you get angry? Do you become controlling? Do you blame someone? Do you laugh? Do you cry? Do you give up and let things go where they will?

- Once I dreamt of a woman wound in barbed wire, set on a slowly revolving chair in a storefront window. The wire cut across her skin, across her lips, keeping them closed. In the dream, I could hear her internal monologue, as she narrated the story of how she ended up this way. Later, I understood this was an image of silencing. Write your own version of a silenced character. How is your dream character bound? What is their internal monologue?

- Sometimes, if I fall asleep while reading a novel, I will dream in the voice of the novel. It is both the author's presence and the narrator's presence and the voice of the novel itself. When this happens, it is as if the book is inside of me, making its way through me on a cellular level. A new story, the pace and color of it, came to me after I fell asleep reading Sarah Shun Lien Bynum's *Madeline Is Sleeping,* and dreamt in the novel's voice. It was sepia and quiet and ancient, twelve blindfolded girls working in a cellar kitchen. For many months, I had only the idea of this dream until my story began to speak to me out of these nuances. It was as if Bynum's story woke mine up. Try letting another writer's voice enter your dreams by intentionally reading before a nap. Invite the book to infiltrate your imagination. If it helps, choose a good sentence from the book to think about as you doze.

- Listen carefully and borrow language from your own family, your own culture, from other lives. Take one tiny scene from this culture and slow it down, write it out.

- Write physical pain.

- Listen to jazz or blues or rock or medieval or global music very loudly. Write about a character listening to the same music and see what happens to them.

- Know the kind of writing that electrifies you with interest. Pull out a text you love. Study the parts of it that especially please you. Copy out a paragraph/section/set of lines. Think about it. Think about it again. Count the words. Look at the parts of the sentences. See what literary tools are at play. Pull out your favorite words and look at them alone on a page. What can you learn from this author, this text that will inform your own writing?

- Riff with your pen and start writing about your earliest memories of reading or of being read to. Write about books you loved. Write about anything you've re-read. Write about what you read now. Don't imagine an audience for this. This is between you and your reader self.

- Take any five books and rant about them or praise them in 300-500 words. Write about re-reading books. Write about hardbacks or paperbacks or e-books, or audio books. Do these different modes affect you differently as a reader? Do you love cliffhangers? Do you read the endings before you have finished the book?

- In Mary Oliver's book, *Upstream,* she writes about creative interruptions:

  > But just as often, if not more often, the interruption comes not from another but from the self itself, or some other self within the self, that whistles and pounds upon the door panels and tosses itself, splashing, into the pond of meditation. And what does it have to say? That you must phone the dentist, that you are out of mustard, that your uncle Stanley's birthday is two weeks hence. You react, of course. Then you return to your work, only to find that the imps of idea have fled back into the mist.

  The next time you are interrupted from your creativity, pay attention to what your internal distractions are. Is there hunger? Text messages? Is it straightening the house? Doing laundry? Going out for lunch? Shopping? How do you bring your attention back to your writing? How do you call back Oliver's "imps of idea"?

- Write out a classic imagined doom that you indulge in but control it and make it work for you by giving it to a character or imagined narrator. (For example: Someone drives off the road in an ice storm, someone is sick with cancer, someone is at the funeral of a beloved, drowning in a river, electrocuted in the tub, etc.)

- Choosing extremely formal language and five-dollar words, or using broken syntax and slang, write about something in your house that irritates you. Choose one of these modes and try it out on a character.

- There's an article in *New York Magazine* by Boris Kachka in 2012, and the article is titled, "Who is the Author of Toni

Morrison?" It's an evocative article discussing Morrison's birth name, but I would like to propose that you answer this question for yourself or for a character. Who is the author of you?

- Write a character who cusses unabashedly.

- One of your characters is obsessed with EXIT signs or something similarly inanimate. Write the origin story of the obsession.

- Choose a character from a text you are reading/writing and compose a section where the character's voice radically slips from its norm. (Say, a pirate begins to speak of Wedgewood china.)

- One of your characters witnesses a car accident. Describe the experience in detail and what effect it has on the character.

- Rewrite a specific major event in human history and give it a different outcome.

- "True stories are nourishing. They feed us," writes Philip Pullman in *His Dark Materials*. Think of a story that you love. Write about what kinds of nourishment this story offers you.

- One of your characters is lying in bed. Write about them imagining themselves from a camera above their bed, and then zoom out to the street, zoom out to the city, zoom out to the state, zoom out to the continent. Does this comfort or alarm your character?

- Write a portrait of a character's intellectual, physical, emotional, spiritual life.

Self-portrait

- Write about someone (real or fictive, familiar, or stranger) imagining you. Think about what tone their thoughts might take (loving, bitter, curious).

- Write a story based on someone in your family about whom there are many family stories, good or bad. Have this character arrive somewhere, in some form, perhaps they arrive in a boat, or it's their voice on the telephone, or they walk into a room. Use real family stories or invent one.

- What images, if you had to choose, say, five-ten recurring or powerful images, would you choose to explore your own (or a character's) cultural, familial, or personal lineage? Edwidge Danticat uses braids, gardens, recitations, fire, spirits, women, babies, blood. Selah Saterstrom uses bones, floorboards, flowers, sisters, and the color blue. For a specific character in a novel, I used helmets, coffee, stars, hands, dust. Once you've made a list, take any one of these isolated images and write a paragraph either specifically about the image, or with the narrator/ character experiencing the image.

- Write about something you don't want to say aloud to your doctor and explain why.

- Write about something that is considered "fun" that you dread and describe the history of this dread.

- Write a story about a culture that you are descended from and know well. Experiment with using any dialects or colloquialism or rules that occur in this culture. Or do this for a character. (Southern drawl, Spanglish, aphorisms, etc.)

- Write about a specific food that symbolizes each member of your family. Write about the dishes and find connections to personality traits.

- Write a self-portrait of your intellectual, physical, emotional, spiritual life.

- Noting your likes and dislikes about a house, about a restaurant, about a friend, about your town, about a teacher or mentor, about a gas station, a convenience store can be an interesting practice. These are small ways to get in the practice of observing yourself, analyzing your habits and methods and obsessions. Write about one of these likes or dislikes with yourself as the narrator, and then write it again as a character's likes or dislikes.

- Write about something you can do for hours straight.

- Answer the following for yourself or a character you have created: Where does truth reside? In your brain? Heart? Describe where you hold truth. To whom do you lie? To whom do you always speak the truth? Is truth possible in memory? Is the opposite of a lie always a truth? Are there absolute truths?

- Name four things you want to write about but believe that you shouldn't. Name the "editors" who block this writing or any reasons why you will not write of these things.

- Think of your favorite writer or your favorite painter, your favorite singer. Your favorite guitarist. Your favorite animator. Or think of someone whose work either inspires or infuriates you. Think of this person's work, and ask *Why Make That?* Answer the question in terms of ways that their work changed, illuminated, thrilled, or angered you as a recipient.

- What is a room? Walls and a floor and a ceiling. These are significant places that hold the events and atmospheres of your existence. Think of places where you've lived, sorrowed, celebrated, written. In these places I remember my gestures of desperation and my moments of luxury. Once in a grant application, I was asked to respond to a prompt about Virginia Woolf's room of one's own. I detailed a desk in a closet, one at the edge of a tiny bedroom, one in my grandfather's study with its rusty paperclips. What this writing illustrated is that life doesn't stop for writing, but I always made space for it. Think about the act of housing your desire to write, putting a roof over your texts, tucking your imagination into a place where it will be safe and cared for. The idea of the writing space is paramount, precious. Describe a perfect realistic room for your writing if money or location were no object. Describe a perfect magical room if you could create one anywhere on the planet or in the cosmos.

- Write out the strengths and weaknesses you think are present in one of your texts. (Different texts challenge us in different ways. These are not permanent victories or afflictions.) Use specific terms relating to what comes easily to you (dialogue, pacing) and what you specifically want to work on in the coming days (action scene vs. summary, characterization).

- What is one of your worst fears/flaws? Name it in a word or a phrase. For example, I fear that I am a burden. In my book, *The Grief Manuscript*, the Burden Animal manifests with bulbous body parts and claws and yellow eyes. How might your fear/flaw manifest as an animal or an insect or a monster (or this monster might be part animal or insect).

- Take five nouns that are near you right now. (Sprinkler, empty bowl, prescription bottle, cup of cold coffee, book.) What is your most essential mood this week? Depressed? Delighted? Angry? Deadened? Try writing five sentences where these objects are described in a way that reveals this mood.

- Talk to yourself about your hopes for your writing. Do you want to be a person who writes in a journal? Do you want to be a poet? Do you want to be a short story writer? Do you want to write nonfiction? Do you want to write stories of redemption? Mystery stories? Horror stories? Romances? Literary stories? Science fiction? Let your hopes be seen on the page.

- Write a description of yourself (or a character) as a body of water. Are you still? Are you moving? Are you massive? Are you a droplet? Are you gushing? Are you poisoned? Are you fresh? Are you saltwater? Go to the place where you are water and write from there.

- If you dream of publishing a book someday, spend some time imagining a book you might write. What genre is it? What kind of cover? How many pages? Who writes the blurb? Are there any similar recent titles?

- Write a detailed description of a place where you have spent time alone with your imagination. In my early twenties, I lived in a beige one-bedroom apartment in a beige apartment complex with my boyfriend. We had a narrow walk-in closet full of clothes, my boyfriend's on one side, mine on the other. Under my hangers full of thrifted sweaters, skirts, and shirts, I set up a large cardboard box and covered it with a red, patterned scarf. I couldn't shut the door because of the plug for my computer, but I sat in front of the box on a straight-backed chair. The whole box shook when I wrote. The closet was airless, and the shoes exuded a leathery musk. When I looked down, they seemed a host of little animals with open mouths. It was hard to think in this closet, but I wouldn't admit it because it was the only privacy I could find. I wrote a page in a notebook in that closet that I have returned to again and again over the years because it still inspires me. Rather than obsessing about a better place for writing, I went ahead and wrote. Write about a place where you write, write about what you write there.

- Go back to any subject matter that you've studied that interested you. Use the techniques that people use to learn or implement that subject matter to create writing prompts for yourself. Say you love studying chemistry. You might use elements and a procedure to solve problems in chemistry. Take two (emotional) elements (isolation and yearning) and a procedure (scene with dialogue and interior monologue) and write a new moment into the world. Or you could write a scene where characters try to solve a problem in chemistry.

- Say you love learning about color in an art class. Write some abstract lines or a story where each character is simply a color.

- Describe a character watching what happens outside their window every day.

- In "A Theory of Human Motivation," psychologist Abraham Maslow theorized that human decision-making is undergirded by a hierarchy of psychological needs. Every single human reading this book can relate to these needs. Take each one as a prompt. Write at least a page about yourself or a character for each need. Specifics shine.

  1. Physiological needs: Food, water, shelter, clothing, health.
  2. Safety needs: Protection emotional stability and well-being, finances, from violence and theft.
  3. Love and belonging needs: Human interactions are the last of the so-called lower needs. Among these needs are friendships and family bonds—both with biological family (parents, siblings, children) and chosen family (spouses and partners). Physical and emotional intimacy ranging from sexual relationships to intimate emotional bonds are important to achieving a feeling of elevated kinship.
  4. Esteem needs: The primary elements of esteem are self-respect (the belief that you are valuable and deserving of dignity) and self-esteem (confidence in your potential for personal growth and accomplishments).
  5. Self-actualization needs: Self-actualization describes the fulfillment of your full potential as a person. Self-actualization needs include education, skill development—the refining of talents in areas such as music, athletics, design, cooking, and gardening—caring for others, and broader goals like learning a new language, traveling to new places, and winning awards.

Craft Techniques

- Sum up a story or text you have written in one sentence. For example: *A man calls a sin eater to abolish his sins and makes her some meals.*

- Go to books on your shelves and find love scenes. Copy passages that you like out by hand. Take notes beneath these passages about elements that surprise you, in content, sentence structure, punctuation, pacing, etc.

- Write the heart of each scene in the margin of your text. For example: *Aggi almost dies. Aggi recovers. Aggi despairs.*

- Create a family of characters at a table. They are discussing a major issue that will affect them all in some way. Use each characters point of view in successive paragraphs to explore how each character thinks and speaks about the issue.

- If you are struggling with a short story ending, write out the last paragraph of five of your favorite short stories. Writing a novel ending? Write out the last paragraph of five of your favorite novels. Writing a novel opening? Write out the first paragraph of five of your favorite novels. You get the idea. There's a lot of scrabble and murk about imitation, but here, you let these mentors guide you, offer you options.

- Write a paragraph of text. Now add at least five footnotes that give additional information or add to the plot, character development, or theme of the story.

- Look through your files, digital or paper. Select a medical or other receipt or certificate. Write a letter in response (a crazed or inappropriate or confessional or furious or pathetic response) to the office or certifier. OR write a letter to someone else regarding the information in the receipt.

- Write a third person story about a family using the tags: *father mother brother sister grandmother* to achieve a mythic distance.

- In first person, write the interior monologue of a date that is not going well. (Any kind of date between any people having lunch, coffee, married, etc.)

- Write a second person point of view description of having something prepared for you. (A meal, a ritual, a bed, a lesson, a conversation.)

- Write from your own burning moments. Write out an intense scene for a character but use your own experience to fuel the emotional subtext. Write a fight, a sex scene, a moment of irrevocable revelation. Cast off your editors and your sense of perfection or politeness. Go all the way out on a limb. Use your own fury or love or sorrow or yearning to inform this scene.

- How would you describe the overall tone of the three pieces of work you have written? List each and name a main tone. Add a secondary tone, too, if you think of one. (Tone, in a piece of literature, decides how the readers are being directed to read a piece, and signifies how they should feel while they are reading it. Is it serious, funny, far out, or upsetting?)

- Do you know what your predilection for conflict is in your own texts? Do you tend towards one most of the time or do you have multiple conflicts in your texts? Write down a conflict from your own life, either now or in the past, that influences your choice of conflict.

    1. Person against Person
    2. Person against Self
    3. Person against Nature
    4. Person against Society
    5. Person against the Supernatural
    6. Person against Technology

- Writer-to-character: Interrogate a character from one of your texts where they explain to you, the author, why a certain conflict arose for them. As the author, explain to the character why you wrote that certain conflict for them. This could either be each of you offering a monologue, or it could be written as back-and-forth dialogue. Examine the two accounts for similarities and differences.

- Write a conversation where a relationship ends (love, friendship, work). This can be detailed with dialogue and gestures and setting, or it can be summarized dialogue and made abstract with just a few sensory observations of the setting offered by a narrator.

- How many intense scenes does your piece have in how many pages of text? Is there balance?

- Think of yourself in third person while you move through the world and write it down. If I'm on a plane, then I might think: There is a writer on a plane, and she watches the sun rise in orange and red filters of clouds on the horizon. This writer spends the night outside of Amsterdam. For a time, she is a woman riding shuttles and trains into Amsterdam Centraal, where people whiz by on bikes and the canal shines up. In a tavern, the writer meets a young German woman who is also traveling alone, and they share a plate of fried potatoes and cheese while a stray cat twines herself between their legs. Tall candles on the tables flicker as bicycles clatter by. The women drink yellow beer from large glasses and talk about the books they are reading and the places they will travel until they rise and say goodbye. The writer sleeps in a small single bed in a hotel in Hoofdorf, which the hotel clerk tells her in accented English, is a nowhere town.

- Write a letter from a failing body part to the owner of the body. Diatribe or love letter or both.

- Begin a story with something that has been lost. This could be metaphorical or literal. For example, a stolen car, a lost limb, a deceased mother, a lost innocence, a lost faith, a lost heart, a lost dream, a lost key. After opening with this, use flashbacks to tell the story of how this loss happened.

- Think of two or three of your texts and their themes. What are they trying to communicate about human experience? Is there a common theme?

- In *Labyrinths*, Jorge Borges writes, "I do not know which of us has written this page." I love the mystery of this question, the tantalizing possibility that authors have more than one life inside of them. I get help from characters I've written. Sometimes I'm advised by a circus ringmaster or a forensic pathologist. What internal resources do you have?

• Every cell in the body writes the book, lives the life. Every cell in the body wants the body's success. Write an ode to the cells in your body that make your writing possible.

• "Emotions do not grow old." —Eudora Welty in *One Writer's Beginnings.*

  Write about an emotion you've had that is still as bright and sharp as you first experienced it, whether it is positive or negative. Write a few sentences describing the quality of this moment in real life. Next, imagine it in a character—either someone you know, or someone you invent—and give this person the emotion instead. Intense emotions can lead to revelations.

• Try writing from the Super Present Tense. This is a way to practice holding a moment, by immersing yourself in the sensory (smell, taste, touch, sight, hearing) action of a single minute of time. Study the details for the ones you want to emphasize, and decide which details are unimportant. Do you want an atmosphere? An emotion? A set-up for something, or simply a moment in-and-of itself? Just start writing. Try using your senses and whatever thoughts you might want to grab out of the air around you. A feeling or understanding or concept might emerge. Write that down, too, if it comes. For example: I have both feet up on the wing chair, my back on the thick blue rug. My grey cat is beside me, and I have one hand on his fur. The air conditioning clicks on and flows

over us. I can see the silver clock and it is 4:00 pm, a nowhere
time, a nothing time, an in-between time for us. We lie on
the rug and wait.

Or I might imagine the same thing for a character: Aggi's
fingers are wrapped on her teacup. The hummingbirds buzz
and chirr in the courtyard. She stares at her brother's shaking
hands. He turns a page in his book and the paper rattles. She
realizes that his hands might never stop shaking, the rattled
pieces inside of him too broken to mend. A horse clops by.

- Make lists. Choose something that appears on the list and
write a detailed scene around it.

Some Things I've Written Upon:
1. Receipt tape from registers
2. Folded looseleaf in back pockets
3. Sheaths of flattened cardboard in an inventory room
4. The blank page in backs of books
5. The back flaps of books
6. Tiny notebooks
7. Spiral notebooks
8. Expensive notebooks
9. Cheap notebooks
10. Recycled, yellowed, fresh, lined, and unlined notebooks
11. Old order forms
12. Cocktail napkins at the bar between shifts
13. Paper candy bar wrappers
14. Receipts from the wallet
15. Paper ads that fall from magazines
16. Postcards you meant to send
17. Old music notation paper

18. Old library Dewey decimal cards
19. Forming words on a leg, with a finger, for memorization
20. In acronyms, also for memorization: "The little organ is a dream." "Dream Organ." "D.O."

Some Places Where I've Written:
1.   Under the hedge in Chestnut Hill
2.   In the lunchroom
3.   On their broken chair in the garden
4.   Next to a wheelchair with a woman in it
5.   Beside his easel
6.   Sitting on sand
7.   Sitting on rocks
8.   Sitting on curbs
9.   Sitting on counters
10. Sitting on benches
11. Knees up, in bed
12. Next to 400 suitcases in an attic
13. In the empty bar before intermission
14. On the truck
15. In the hallways
16. On the edge of the stage
17. On the sides of mountains
18. In kayaks
19. Next to the receiving belt
20. In the lunchroom
21. In the lunchroom
22. In the lunchroom
23. In the cleaning closet, waiting for the mop bucket to fill
24. In her borrowed basement
25. In libraries

26. In cafes

27. In other countries

28. In someone else's kitchen

29. In the hospital waiting rooms

30. In my grandfather's abandoned study

31. On a box in the closet

32. Upstairs, with that ghost rushing around

33. On trains

34. On porches

35. On planes

For more prompts, webinars, and one-on-one coaching,
sign up for the Fifth Brain Collective newsletter at
fifthbraincollective.com.

Acknowledgments

Thanks to Superstition Review's [S]r blog/vlog where some of this work was published as "How I Got on the Wrong Bus," "I Lost a Manuscript: A Particular Silence," "I am an Animal Text," and "The Work."

Thanks to these folks who celebrate the fifth brain: Sandra Shattuck, Eric Aldrich, Beth Laking, Kristen Nelson, Selah Saterstrom, Christine Simokaitis, Kirsten Rybzcinski, Kye Davolt, GFK, TC Tolbert, Rosie Perera, Samantha Bounkeua, Hannah Ensor, Kimi Eisele, HR Hegnauer, Dawn Paul, Eva Hayward, Timothy Dyke, Mary Page Jones, Bobby G. Jones, Mary Murphy Irvine, John Irvine, Raymond Rollins, Christine Rollins, Howard Grahn, Felicia Shakman, Victor Valdivia, Alison Climes, Jenna Korsmo, Diana Jaramillo, Maggie Golston, Jill Brammer, Hannah Levin, Jill Steinhauser, Sacha Steinhauser, Marilyn Keating, Debra Sachs, Rebecca Brown, Chris Galloway, Kathleen Wallace, and in memoriam, Sy Platt.

Gratitude to Cyane, Jake, and Leo Tornatzky in Fort Collins, Colorado, for the welcome, meals, games, and dreamy writing space in the pottery shed.

Gratitude to Peter and Rea Busch, who loaned me their flat in Latchi, Cyprus for five weeks of writing time for the first draft of this book.

Thanks to Pima Community College in Tucson, AZ for a semester sabbatical to draft this book.

Love to all the writers who allowed me passage into their writing process so that I knew how to write this book.

One last story that holds my wish for you, reader: As a teaching artist conducting a week of workshops in a New

Jersey elementary school, I offered an exercise in figurative language to a fourth-grade class. I was walking around the room, unsticking the stuck brains, celebrating with others, when a boy I'd been told was a "troublemaker" abruptly stood at his desk, still writing furiously. He called out the uncanny metaphors he was scribbling and tossed the sheets of paper, one after another, triumphantly to the floor. The class fell silent, and we participated in his illumination with our astonishment. This young writer called out one last metaphor and tossed it with a flourish. We clapped and hooted. Other students stood to hug him and offer high-fives. He turned to stare me
in the eye, a fierce grin on his face, as if to say, *This belongs to me now.*

About the Author

Frankie Rollins is the author of three works of fiction, *The Grief Manuscript*, *The Sin Eater & Other Stories,* and *Doctor Porchiat's Dream.* Originally advertising her classes with a sandwich board at a farmer's market in 2001, Frankie has taught creative writing in import stores, living rooms, coffeeshops, florists, K-12 classrooms, and in scores of college classrooms, traditional and online. In 2023, Frankie launched the Fifth Brain Collective, offering imaginative writing coaching, innovative classes, and an online community platform for writers.

Sign up for Frankie's newsletter at frankierollins.com.

* 9 7 9 8 9 8 8 1 9 3 7 0 8 *